CMOS Simplified:

The Chicago Manual of Style 17th Made Easy

Full Student's Guide to Chicago Style

Student Citation Styles Series

Appearance Publishers
2022

CMOS Simplified: The Chicago Manual of Style 17th Made Easy
Full Student's Guide to Chicago Style
1st Edition
Copyright © 2022 Appearance Publishers
All rights reserved.
ISBN: 978-1-4716-7046-6

CMOS Simplified: The Chicago Manual of Style 17th Made Easy
Full Student's Guide to Chicago Style

Student Citation Styles Series
Book 16

"CMOS Simplified: The Chicago Manual of Style 17th Made Easy" is specifically designed for students and professional writers to quickly learn updated Chicago Style in a convenient and easy way both Notes and Bibliography referencing system and Author-Date referencing system.

Revised according to the latest edition of The Chicago Manual of Style (17th ed.), this guide is offering guidelines, general formats, and examples of paper layout, running head, title page, contents, abstract, appendixes, headings, lists, numbers, tables and illustrations, text styling, punctuation, abbreviations, bias-free language, in-text citations (notes: footnotes and endnotes; parenthetical citations), quotations (including changes to quotations), bibliography/reference list including Chicago sample paper.

Cite any type of work using general formats and examples of 100+ sources divided into categories (books, articles in periodicals, reviews, encyclopedias and dictionaries, websites, social media, audiovisual multimedia, academic sources, personal communication, interviews, government publications, legal sources).

With this guide, you will be able to format your paper according to the Chicago Style right away thanks to its easy-to-navigate structure and step-by-step guidelines on setting up research papers in Chicago format.

Includes bibliographical references.

CONTENTS

1.0 INTRODUCTION

Chicago (The Chicago Manual of Style, Chicago Style, CMOS, CMS)

This guide is based on *The Chicago Manual of Style* (17th edition) and it illustrates the Chicago style general layout, requirement and common formatting for the sources most frequently used by students and professional writers.

Chicago style has developed the following standards:
- Formatting and page layout,
- Stylistic techniques,
- Citing sources, etc.

Advantages of using Chicago style:
- Chicago style provides a well-known structure throughout the paper that allows readers to follow your ideas more efficiently.
- Abiding by Chicago style standard of formatting permits readers to easily locate the sources you refer to.

Chicago style uses **two referencing systems**:

1. **Notes and Bibliography (NB)** Referencing System is used in:	2. **Author-Date (AD)** Referencing System is used in:
<ul><li>Humanities,</li><li>Arts,</li><li>Literature,</li><li>History, etc.</li></ul>	<ul><li>Physical sciences,</li><li>Natural sciences,</li><li>Social sciences, etc.</li></ul>

Two systems are identical in content, but are different in form:

	Notes and Bibliography **(NB)** Referencing System	Author-Date **(AD)** Referencing System
Differences in referencing	<ul><li>Notes and Bibliography (NB) referencing system uses numbered notes in the text to direct the reader to footnotes (citations at the bottom of the page) or endnotes (citations at the end of the paper).</li><li>Each note (footnote or endnote) links to the full entry on the bibliography page at the end of the paper.</li></ul>	<ul><li>Author-Date (AD) referencing system uses parenthetical citations in the text to reference the source (author and the year of publication).</li><li>Each parenthetical citation links to the full entry on a references page at the end of the paper.</li></ul>
Citations within the Text	There is a huge influence of the environment in shaping people's behavior, personality, and perception.[1]<hr>1. James Brooks, Favorite Athlete (New York: Pocket Books, 2018), 43.	There is a huge influence of the environment in shaping people's behavior, personality, and perception (Brooks 2018, 43).
List of Sources	Bibliography Brooks, James. Favorite Athlete. New York: Pocket Books, 2018.	References Brooks, James. 2018. Favorite Athlete. New York: Pocket Books.

Consult your instructor for the preferred referencing system.

This guide will address the vast majority of questions about using Chicago style correctly both:
1. Notes and Bibliography referencing system and
2. Author-Date referencing system.

Additionally, this guide includes guidelines from Kate L. Turabian's *Manual for Writers of Research Papers, Theses, and Dissertations* for student papers.

Keep in mind: your instructor is the final authority on how to format your paper correctly.

Appearance Publishers
2021

2.0 IMPORTANT CHANGES IN THE 17TH EDITION

Changed guidelines:
- Instead of using "ibid" to cite the same source, Chicago style prefers to use shortened notes.
- When citing online sources from database, provide the database name instead of URL.
- Always capitalize the first word of a direct question, even in the middle of the sentence.
- The use of "US" as a noun is now allowed.
- Do not use a comma after "etc." for items in a series.
- Do not capitalize "internet."
- Do not hyphenate "email."
- Do not use "Ms. President" or "Mrs. President"; instead use "Madam President."
- Do not italicize "Wikipedia" and other online reference works with no print version.
- Within AD referencing system, for periodicals with month, day, and year of publication, repeat the year twice to avoid ambiguity.

New guidelines (covered in this guide as well)**:**
- New guidelines on formatting abstracts and keywords.
- New guidelines on formatting lists including:
  - Capitalization of the first items in bulleted / numbered list.
- New guidelines on formatting numbers (commas / periods / spaces within digits) including:
  - Use of ratios.
  - Use of spaces with numbers and units of measurement.
  - Plurals of units of measurement.
  - Format of telephone numbers.
- New guidelines on formatting tables.
- New guidelines on emphasis (italics / boldface / underscore).
- New guidelines on punctuation with "too."
- New guidelines on agreement of indefinite pronouns (anyone / everyone).
- New guidelines on agreement of pronouns joined by "either ... or" and "neither ... nor"
- New guidelines on using bias-free and inclusive language including:
  - Use of "they."
- New guidelines on styling titles of:
  - Rhymes,
  - Fairy tales,
  - Video games,
  - Maps,
  - Applications, devices, operating systems.
- New guidelines on introducing quotations.
- New guidelines on line breaks within quotations.
- New guidelines on styling "the" at the beginning of newspapers and journals.
- New guidelines on citing:
  - Locations in electronic sources with no fixed pages.
  - Social media posts and comments.
  - Images (photographs, paintings, sculptures, maps, etc.).
  - Live performances.

3.0 GENERAL GUIDELINES

3.1 Paper Layout

Chicago style has the following requirements for the paper layout:
- Use standard paper, A4 format:
  - 8.5 inches x 11 inches.
- Set **margins** between 1 and 1.5 inches on all sides of the page.
- The text is **double-spaced** throughout the paper **except** for:
  - Block quotations
  - Notes (endnotes / footnotes)
  - Bibliography / Reference list
  - Table and illustration captions
- Justify the text at the **left margin only** (with a "ragged" right edge):
  - The first line of every paragraph is **indented** 0.5 inches.
- Use readable fonts, such as:
  - Times New Roman
  - Courier, etc.
- Set font size between 10 and 12 pt.
- Leave one empty line between notes and bibliography/reference list.
- Use **one space** between words:
  - Leave only one space after period as well.
- Do not use automatic hyphenation feature for your text at the end of lines:

Example of Paper Layout:

The paper should consist of the following major sections (arranged in **this order**):

1. Title page
2. Dedication (if using)
3. Contents (if using)
4. List of Illustrations (if using)
5. List of Tables (if using)
6. Abstract (if using)
7. Acknowledgments (if using)
8. Main Body pages
9. Appendixes (if using)
10. Endnotes (if using)
11. Bibliography/References

3.2 Running Head and Pagination

Running head (header) is the text line that appears at the **top of every page**.

- In Chicago style, the running head contains the **page number**:
  - Justify the number to the right:

Example:
1

- If instructed by your institution, include your **last name**:

Example:
Johnson 1

- Do not use running head for the front matter (title page, dedication, contents, etc.).
- Start using running head from the **first page of the main body**:
  - Use Arabic numerals beginning with 1.
- Do not use running head for pages that contain only illustrations or tables.

If instructed, use **special** running head for the front matter (except title page):
- For page numbers, use Roman numerals beginning with ii:
  - The title page is counted as i even though it does not contain running head:

Example:
ii

Summary

Paper Section	Running Head Usage
1. Title page	NEVER USE
2. Dedication 3. Contents 4. List of Illustrations 5. List of Tables 6. Abstract 7. Acknowledgments	USE IF INSTRUCTED: Roman numerals starting from ii
8. Main Body pages 9. Appendixes 10. Endnotes 11. Bibliography/References	ALWAYS USE: Arabic numerals starting from 1

3.3 Major Paper Sections

Title Page

The title page (cover page) takes the full first page of paper:
- Do not use running head or page number for the title page.
- The title page is **double-spaced**.
- Center the title of paper 1/3 of the way down the page:
  - o Place subtitle on the next line and use a colon after the title.
  - o Use **ALL CAPS** for both title and subtitle.
- Center your name, class information, and date 2/3 of the way down the page:
  - o If instructed by your institution, include the instructor's name or any other information.
  - o Place each item on a new line:

General Format:	*Example:*
TITLE OF PAPER: SUBTITLE OF PAPER Your Name Class Information Date	SOCIAL ACTION: WRITING AND PERFORMANCE AS PATH Oliver Johnson Sociology 224: Sociology, Social Psychology January 16, 2020

Contents

ontents (table of contents) is used for papers **divided into chapters** or the like:
- Include contents only **if instructed** by your institution.
- Contents is placed on a **separate page**.
- Do not list material that precedes contents.
- List all major paper sections that follow contents:
    1. List of Illustrations (if using)
    2. List of Tables (if using)
    3. Abstract (if using)
    4. Acknowledgments (if using)
    5. Main Body pages
    6. Appendixes (if using)
    7. Endnotes (if using)
    8. Bibliography/References
- Provide **headings** and respective **page numbers** of paper sections:
    o Subheadings can usually be omitted from contents.

Chicago style does not provide more specific instructions on formatting contents:
- Follow the guidelines set by your institution or follow the example below:

Example:

ii

Contents

Abstract   iv
Acknowledgments v
Introduction   1

PART I HEADING

1 Heading 3
2 Heading 8
    2.1 Subheading 10
    2.2 Subheading 12

PART II HEADING

1 Heading 14
2 Heading 17

Conclusion   21
Appendixes   23
Bibliography   26

Abstract

The abstract is a **concise summary** of the key points of the paper:
- The abstract usually contains **150–200 words**.
- The abstract is placed on a **separate page**:
  - Use a **single paragraph**.
  - **Do not indent** the first line of paragraph.
  - Do not include lists, notes, citations, tables, illustrations, etc.
- The abstract provides paper's main arguments and conclusions.
- As an option, use **5–10 keywords** at the end of abstract:
  - For each keyword, use a single word or a compound of few words.

Chicago style does not provide more specific instructions on formatting abstract:
- Follow the guidelines set by your institution or follow the general ones:
  - Begin the abstract on a separate page.
    - Center and bold "Abstract."
    - Leave two blank lines before the text of your abstract begins.
  - Your abstract should:
    - Be double-spaced.
    - Be single not indented paragraph.
    - Contain no more than 250 words.
  - Additionally, you may list paper's keywords:
    - Indent the first line 0.5 inches after the abstract paragraph.
    - Italicize "Keywords:".
    - Add 5–10 keywords in lowercase letters, not italicized, separated with commas.
    - Do not use a period after the final keyword.

Example:

iii

Abstract

Lorem ipsum dolor sit amet, consectetur adipiscing elit. Nullam suscipit consequat dui, et luctus ante iaculis quis. Cras facilisis rhoncus velit a varius. Nunc metus sapien, vehicula in felis in, dapibus cursus lorem. Proin condimentum sagittis suscipit. Luctus ac mauris. Vestibulum sed erat non massa porta ultricies eu nec elit. Duis ut tellus elit. Aenean varius imperdiet lorem, et dictum mi commodo vitae. Donec sit amet dictum est. Sed at sem mattis, bibendum urna ac, gravida neque. Morbi accumsan metus eu velit fermentum, ut elementum ex blandit. Nulla nec nibh felis. Proin facilisis condimentum scelerisque. Sed congue lorem in ullamcorper consectetur. Nullam dapibus, elit quis tincidunt scelerisque, diam orci porttitor turpis, eu malesuada justo eros sed augue. Pellentesque nec rutrum risus. Vestibulum condimentum tincidunt mi, at commodo eros suscipit ut. Mauris condimentum maximus sem. Vivamus sed arcu eget erat vulputate imperdiet vel vel massa. Vestibulum sed dignissim nisl. Aenean libero felis, lobortis.

Keywords: Ipsum, purus, pulvinar, porttitor, consectetur

Appendixes

An appendix (or appendixes) may be included to allow readers **better understand** the material in case there is a need to provide clarification or additional content that may not fit within the main text of paper:

- Transcripts of conducted interviews.
- Documents (survey questionnaires, tests, results, etc.).
- Long lists.
- Detailed statistical data.
- Tables, charts, illustrations, etc.

Appendixes are placed after the last page of the main text:

- Use a **new page** for each appendix.
- Label "Appendix" is placed at the top of the page:
  - Centered and bolded.
- Label "Appendix" is followed by a number or letter to distinguish between appendixes:
  - Appendix 1, Appendix 2, Appendix 3, etc.
  - Appendix A, Appendix B, Appendix C, etc.
- Label "Appendix" is also followed by a title on the next line:
  - Title gets headline-style capitalization.
  - Centered, not bolded.
- As an option, appendixes may be set in **smaller font**:

Example:

36

Appendix 1

Title of the Appendix

3.4 Headings

Chicago style does not provide specific instructions on formatting headings with the paper; however, it recommends:
- Develop your **own format** for headings:
  - Maintain the styling of headings consistently.
- Use subheadings for longer papers:
  - To distinguish between heading levels, style the headings in descending order of prominence.
  - To signal prominence, use different styling, size, and placement on the page.
- Maintain **hierarchy** of heading levels **consistent**:
  - Use up to 3 heading levels.
- Use **headline-style capitalization** for headings.
- Do use periods at the end of headings.

Alternatively, use Turabian style guidelines to style headings:

Turabian System of 5 Heading Levels

	General Format:
Level 1	**Centered, Bold, Headline-Style Capitalization** Text starts with a new paragraph.
Level 2	Centered, Regular, Headline-Style Capitalization Text starts with a new paragraph.
Level 3	*Flush Left, Italics or Bold, Headline-Style Capitalization* Text starts with a new paragraph.
Level 4	Flush left, regular, sentence-style capitalization Text starts with a new paragraph.
Level 5	*Indented, italics or bold, sentence-style capitalization with a period.* Text starts on the same line/paragraph as the heading.

Example:	**Global Pollution** Text starts with a new paragraph... Air and Atmosphere Text starts with a new paragraph... *Pollution Source* Text starts with a new paragraph... Human-made pollution Text starts with a new paragraph... *Cars and other vehicles.* Text starts on the same line/paragraph as the heading... *Factories.* Text starts on the same line/paragraph as the heading...

Numbered Headings

For scientific and technical papers, use numeration to distinguish between different heading levels.
- Use multilevel numeration:
  - Each heading number consists of its higher divisions' numbers separated by:
    - period (.)
    - colon (:)
    - hyphens (-)

Example:	1 Chapter Heading
	   1.1 Section Heading
	   1.2 Section Heading
	      1.2.1 Subsection Heading
	      1.2.2 Subsection Heading
	   1.3 Section Heading
	2 Chapter Heading
	   2.1 Section Heading
	   2.2 Section Heading

Headline-Style Capitalization

DO CAPITALIZE	Don't capitalize
<ul><li>Nouns</li><li>Pronouns</li><li>Verbs</li><li>Adjectives</li><li>Adverbs</li><li>Subordinating conjunctions:<ul><li>That</li><li>If</li><li>As If</li><li>As Soon As</li><li>Although</li><li>Because</li><li>Unless</li><li>Till</li><li>Until</li><li>How</li><li>When</li><li>Where</li><li>While</li><li>Who</li><li>Why</li><li>Before</li><li>After</li></ul></li></ul>	<ul><li>Articles:<ul><li>a</li><li>an</li><li>the</li></ul></li><li>Coordinating conjunctions:<ul><li>and</li><li>or</li><li>but</li><li>nor</li><li>yet</li><li>for</li><li>so</li></ul></li><li>Prepositions:<ul><li>between</li><li>against</li><li>according to</li><li>to</li><li>in</li><li>at</li><li>on</li><li>of</li><li>as</li></ul></li><li>The infinitive "to"</li></ul>

3.5 Lists

Lists can be integrated into the sentence (run-in lists) or set vertically (vertical lists):
1. **Short lists** are usually presented as run-in lists.
2. **Long lists** or lists with multiple levels are better presented as vertical lists.

Run-in Lists

It is preferable to integrate lists into the text if the **items are short**:
- To introduce a run-in list, use a colon or an introductory phrase.
- Use **numerals or letters** enclosed in **parentheses** to mark the items within a run-in list:
  - As an option, italicize the letters within parentheses.
- Punctuate items in a run-in list as you would punctuate words in a sentence (usually using commas or semicolons):

Example:	Accessibility and convenience include the following: (1) the broad variety of products and services, (2) online comparison, (3) adequate buildings, (4) basic and urban infrastructure services.
	Accessibility and convenience include (1) the broad variety of products and services, (2) online comparison, (3) adequate buildings, (4) basic and urban infrastructure services.
	Accessibility and convenience include (a) the broad variety of products and services, (b) online comparison, (c) adequate buildings, (d) basic and urban infrastructure services.
	Accessibility and convenience include (*a*) the broad variety of products and services, (*b*) online comparison, (*c*) adequate buildings, (*d*) basic and urban infrastructure services.

Vertical Lists

Vertical lists can be ordered and unordered:
1. In **unordered** vertical lists, items are presented by markers (usually, bullets) or by nothing.
2. In **ordered** vertical lists, items are ordered by numbers or letters.

Introduce vertical list by complete sentence followed by colon:
- Each number and letter is followed **by a period** or other punctuation.
- Each number, letter, and any other marker are followed **by a tab**.

Generally, indent the text following list as a new paragraph:
- Do not indent the text following list if it is a continuation of the paragraph that introduces the list.

Unordered Lists

- **Generally, lowercase** the first letter of each item and use no punctuation at the end of the item.
- For **complete sentences, capitalize** the first letter of each item and use respective punctuation at the end.

No-Marker Lists

- Indent runover lines 0.5 inches:

Example:	Technical surveillance includes the following technical equipment:
	lighting
	CCTV (closed circuit television)
	seismographic sensor technology that is covering the entire range of modern tools such as thermal imaging, laser, and ultrasound
	touch and vibration system
	microwave technology system

- For short items, use several **columns** to arrange items:

Example:	Therefore, the main causes can be established:	
	faulty heath valves	heart arrhythmias
	coronary artery disease	myocarditis
	hypertension	cardiomyopathy

16

- For **complete sentences, capitalize** the first letter of each item and use respective punctuation at the end:
  - Otherwise, **lowercase** the first letter of each item and use **no punctuation** at the end.
- Align runover lines with the first letter of the item:

Example:	Use these conversation topics for the ESL classroom:
	   • Do you dream regularly?
	   • What is a daydream?
	   • What is the difference between our daydreams and our dreams at night?
	   • What is the difference between our everyday life and dreaming while we are sleeping?

Example:	Accessibility and convenience:
	   • the broad variety of products and services
	   • online comparison
	   • adequate buildings
	   • basic and urban infrastructure services

Ordered Lists (Numbered Lists / Lettered Lists)

- Each number and letter is followed **by a period** or other punctuation.
- Always **capitalize** the first letter of each item.
- Use **no punctuation** at the end of item unless they consist of complete sentences.
- Align runover lines with the first letter of the item:

Example:	Accessibility and convenience:
	  1. The broad variety of products and services
	  2. Online comparison
	  3. Adequate buildings
	  4. Basic and urban infrastructure services

Outlines

- Outlines (ordered lists with multiple levels) are presented by **subdivided** items with numbers or letters:

Example:	There are two parts to referencing for each system:
	  1. The citations within the text of your paper
	      1.1. Notes
	      1.2. Parenthetical citations
	  2. An alphabetical list of sources at the end of your paper
	      2.1. Bibliography
	      2.2. References

Vertical Lists as Part of Sentence

For vertical lists that continue an introductory sentence:
- Use no punctuation after the introductory part.
- **Lowercase** the first letter of each item and use commas or semicolons at the end.
- Use **"and"** or **"or"** before the final item.
- Use a period at the end of final item:

Example:	Theodore Collins reported that
	   • the company will be launched in 2022;
	   • the director position is still open; and
	   • the office will be located in New York.

3.6 Numbers

General Guidelines

	Rule	Example
Spell Out	Numbers zero through one hundred *	five twenty-three
	Numbers one through one hundred followed by: • Hundred, thousand, hundred thousand, million, billion, etc.	three hundred sixty-two thousand four hundred million
	Numbers that begin sentences	Nineteen twenty was a time of liberation.
	Simple fractions	two-thirds three quarters
Use Numerals for	Numbers over one hundred	101 938 2,776
	Numbers over one hundred followed by: • Hundred, thousand, hundred thousand, million, billion, etc.	109 thousand 543 million
	Large or complex fractions	8.87
	Fractions followed by: • Hundred, thousand, hundred thousand, million, billion, etc.	1.8 million 67.9 billion
	Numbers with symbols and abbreviations of units of measurement	2 km 17 L 324 g 36.6°C 7'2"
	Monetary amounts with symbols	50¢ $6 $22,000 $6.2 billion
	Percent, %	98% 12.4 percent
	Numbers referring to divisions of books: • Pages, chapters, parts, volumes, tables, figures, etc.	pages 6–19 pages iv–xii part 4 table 19 figures 12–18
Use Numerals + Spell Out	Two numbers placed next to each other: • Spell out the smaller number	15 three-inch cards two 10-foot trees
Use Numerals or Spell Out	Whole numbers + simple fractions	four and one-quarter 9¾
Style Preferences	Use Arabic numerals: • Replace Roman numerals with Arabic numerals	volume 5 chapters 4 and 6
	Omit "and" in numbers	two hundred twenty

* Alternative rule: Spell out "zero through nine" (only single digits).

Additional Guidelines

	Rule	Example
Ordinal Numbers	Apply general rules above to spell or use numerals	second twentieth
	Use full suffixes "st," "nd," "rd," and "th"	eighty-first 103rd
	Do not use superscripts for suffixes	257th
Plural Numbers	For spelled-out numbers, treat them as nouns	eights fifties
	For numerals, add "s" with no apostrophe	the 1950s two 150s
Commas between digits	Use commas between groups of three digits	54,003 9,000,500
	Do not use commas after the decimal marker	0.246793
	Do not use commas for: • Page numbers • Line numbers • Addresses • Years (except years of more than five digits)	page 2095 line 1455 14250 North Eles Avenue April 2012 10,000 BP
Spaces between digits	Use spaces between groups of three digits (instead of commas): • Use such spaces both before and after decimal marker • Do not use such spaces for groups of only four digits	9 000 500 0.246 793 1500.2467
Decimal Marker	Use a period as the decimal marker	55,950.21
Ratios	Spell out or use numerals for ratios: • Use "-to-" for ratios of whole numbers	a five-to-four ratio a 5-to-4 ratio
	As an option, instead of "-to-" use a colon with no spaces around	a 5:4 ratio
Inclusive Numbers (Ranges)	For numerals, use an en dash (–) to express inclusive numbers	pages 29–104
	For spelled-our numbers, use "to" or "-to-" to express inclusive numbers	twenty-nine to fifty-three twenty-to-thirty-year-olds
	"From" is followed by "to," "through," "until"	from 1990 to 2010
	"Between" is followed by "and"	between about 120 and 180

	If the first number...	–	Then, for the second number...	
Abbreviating Inclusive Numbers (Ranges)	Abbreviate inclusive Arabic numbers following the guidelines below:			
	is 1–99	–	use all digits	2–11 62–86 99–109
	ends with "00"	–	use all digits	100–109 2300–2301
	ends with "01" – "09"	–	use changed part only	101–4 607–34 2406–9
	ends with "10" – "99"	–	use changed part (minimum two digits)	156–59 397–402 2287 304 45990–6022
	Write inclusive Roman numerals in full			xiv–xix

	Rule	Example
Simple Fractions	Spell out simple fractions standing alone	two-thirds three quarters
	Spell out or use numerals for whole numbers + simple fractions	four and one-quarter 9¾
Large or Complex Fractions (Fractions with Decimal Marker)	Use numerals for fractions with decimal marker	8.87
	Use numerals for fractions with decimal marker followed by: • Hundred, thousand, hundred thousand, million, billion, etc.	3.6 million 24.3 billion
	For fractions less than 1.00: • Use a zero before the decimal marker • Treat such fractions as plurals	0.29 0.56 people
	For probabilities (or other amounts between −1.00 and 1.00): • Omit a zero before the decimal marker	p < .03
	For firearm calibers: • Omit a zero before the decimal marker	.30-caliber rifle
Units of Measurement	Use numerals for numbers with symbols and abbreviations of units of measurement • Use a space between numbers and abbreviations of units of measurement (km, L, g, etc.) • Use NO space between numbers and symbols of units of measurement (°, %, ', ", etc.)	2 km 17 L 324 g 36.6°C 29% 7'2"
	Use singular form of units of measurement for exactly 1: • Use plural form of units of measurement for ALL other numbers	one inch zero point five inches one point five inches
	For ranges of numbers with units of measurement: • Do not repeat separated from the number unit of measurement • Repeat closed up unit of measurement	10–12 kg 25%–40% 22°C–24°C 8" × 12"
	Spell out units of measurement that appear with no numeral	liter grams
Monetary Amounts	Use numerals for monetary amounts with symbols	50¢ $6
	Do not use spaces between monetary amounts and symbols	$22,000 $22K
	As an option, replace thousands with "K"	$440 million $6.2 billion
Percent, %	Use numerals to express percentages: • Use the word "percent" in nontechnical papers • Use the symbol "%" in scientific papers	23 percent 70% 86.9%
	Do not use spaces between numerals and the symbol "%"	
	For ranges of numerals: • Do not repeat the word "percent" • Repeat the symbol "%"	10–15 percent 40%–49%
Pages, Chapters, Volumes, etc.	Use numerals for numbers referring to divisions of books: • Pages, chapters, parts, volumes, tables, figures, etc.	pages 6–19 pages iv–xii chapter 5 part 4 volume 8 line 1244
Addresses	Apply general rules above to spell or use numerals	Second Avenue Twenty-Third Street
	Follow street numbers with street names	Two Hundred One Estell Drive 435th Street
People Names	Use Roman numerals for parts of people names	Louis XIV Mary II
Telephone Numbers	For the United States and Canada numbers, choose one of the formats and use it consistently throughout the paper	(000) 000-0000 (000) 000-0000, ext. 0000 000-000-0000 1-000-000-0000 (1-000) 000-0000
	For international numbers, use spaces as in the example	+44 20 0000 0000

Dates

	Rule	Example
Years	Use numerals for years	1980
	Spell out years at the beginning of sentences: • Rewrite the sentence so that the year does not begin the sentence	Nineteen twenty was a time of liberation. A time of liberation began in 1920.
	For informal papers, the first two digits can be replaced by apostrophe	the prom of '12
Months and Days	Use cardinal numbers for specific dates: • Use "Month Day, Year" format or • Use "Day Month Year" format	May 30, 2021 30 May 2021
	Spell out dates with no month and year	By the seventeenth, people had left the town.
	In tables, abbreviate months and use "Day Month Year" format if needed	25 Feb 2020
Time	Use numerals to emphasize exact time: • Lowercase and use periods for "a.m." and "p.m."	7:13 a.m. 8:45 a.m. 9:00 p.m. 11:30 p.m.
	Spell out even, half, and quarter hours	eleven thirty half past two a quarter to five
	Spell out hours with "o'clock"	two o'clock
	Spell out noon and midnight: • Use a range of two dates for clarity	by noon at midnight, May 14–15.
	For 24-hour system (if instructed by institution), use four digits: • Punctuation can be omitted	00:05 15:42 24:00 1800 hours 1800 h 0230
Centuries	Spell out, lowercase, and use ordinal numbers or Use numerals + s (no apostrophe)	the nineteenth century the 1800s
Decades	Spell out, lowercase, and use ordinal numbers or Use numerals + s (no apostrophe)	the seventies the 1970s the '70s the first decade of the ninth century
Eras	Use ALL CAPS with no period for eras abbreviations: **Abbreviation** — **Description** BC — Before Christ BCE — Before the common era CE — Common era AD — Anno Domini (in the year of the Lord) AH — Anno Hegirae (in the year of the Hijra) BP — Before present	the eleventh millennium BC 38 BC AD 1005 AH 1255 11,200 BP
	Use BC, BCE, CE, and BP after the year	
	Use AD and AH before the year	
ISO Format	International Organization for Standardization recommends using: • 24-hour system • "Year-Month-Day Hours:Minutes:Seconds" format	2021-12-30 18:45:30.5

3.7 Tables and Illustrations

General Guidelines

Tables and illustrations are **optional visuals** for the paper to structure the information and ease readers' understanding:
- Tables are any graphics that use rows and columns to structure the content.
- Illustrations are any visuals other than tables (photographs, paintings, maps, charts, etc.).

- Position tables and illustrations as soon as possible after they are first referenced:
  - Alternatively, place all tables and illustrations separately in a list of tables and a list of illustrations.
- Captions of tables and illustrations are **single-spaced**:
  - Each caption consists of label, number, and title.
- Cite sources of tables and illustrations with **credit lines** placed at the bottom of tables and illustrations:
  - Use appropriate labels:
    - Data adapted from …
    - Photo by …
  - Use in-text citations format for entries (as in notes or parenthetical citations).
  - Include the source in bibliography/reference list.

Illustrations

Illustrations are any visuals other than tables (photographs, paintings, maps, charts, etc.):
- Follow the same style when presenting illustrations throughout the paper.

Labels:
- Refer to any illustration as **"figure"** or use a specific label ("map" for maps, "chart" for charts, etc.):
  - Refer to musical scores as "examples."

Numbers:
- Number all illustrations **consequently** throughout the paper:
  - If several categories of labels are used, use **separate numeration** for each label (figure 1, figure 2, figure 3, … ; map 1, map 2, map 3, … ; example 1, example 2, example 3, …).
- For scientific papers with chapters, use **double numeration**:
  - Each label consists of the chapter number and the illustration number (figure 6.1, figure 6.2, figure 6.3, …).
- For illustrations that consist of several parts, **assign capital letters** (A, B, C, …) to each part:
  - In text, refer to such parts of illustrations respectively (figure 6.1A, figure 6.1B, figure 6.1C, …).
- For illustrations within appendixes, the number should be preceded by **appendix letter** (A, B, C, …) and a period:
  - (figure A.1, figure A.2, figure A.3, …).

Titles:
- The title should explain what is illustrated:
  - Use a single word, several words, phrase, sentence, or several sentences for the title.
- **Capitalize** the first letter of the title.
- Do not use punctuation at the end of the title if it is incomplete sentence:
  - For complete sentences, use periods at the end.

Captions:
- Each caption consists of label, number, and title of illustration.
- Captions are placed **under** illustrations:
  - Captions of musical scores are placed above.
- Captions are flush left and **single-spaced**.
- Use a period between the number and the title.
- The label "figure" can be abbreviated to "fig.":

Example:	Figure 1. The process of diagnosis
	Figure 2. The increasing number of digital products established value-added structures.
	Fig. 2. The increasing number of digital products established value-added structures.
	Figure 2.1. The increasing number of digital products established value-added structures.

Locators in captions:
- To identify illustrated elements, use special locators ("top," "bottom," "above," "below," "left to right," etc.):
  - Italicize locators.
  - Use comma to introduce a single element.
  - Use colon to introduce several elements:

Example:	Figure 3. *Above left*, James Brooks; *above right*, Violet Wilson; *below right*, Theodore Mitchell

Credit lines:
- Include credit lines **in parentheses** at the end of title:
  - Follow the format of in-text citations for the entries (notes or parenthetical citations):

Example:	Figure 1. Sarah Wells poses for the *Vogue* October issue. (Luna Hall, *Ballet Girl*, August 1998, photograph, *Vogue*, cover, October 1998.)

Callouts:
- In text, provide callouts for each illustration:
  - Use **spelled-out** and **lowercased** labels with numbers (see figure 1, see figure 2, see figure 3, …).
  - The label "figure" can be abbreviated to "fig." when used in parentheses.

Example:	*Example:*
5	7

Aenean a eleifend elit. Class aptent taciti sociosqu ad litora torquent per conubia nostra, per inceptos himenaeos. Nulla ut dolor mi. Suspendisse non maximus nibh. Proin laoreet vel tellus facilisis aliquam. Interdum et malesuada fames ac ante ipsum primis in faucibus. Nulla tempor pretium leo, a suscipit tortor lobortis eget. Integer ac dolor sem.

Figure 1. Guernica is a comparatively late example of Cubism. (Pablo Picasso, *Guernica*, 1937, oil on canvas, 11.5 x 25.6 ft (3.49 x 7.76 m), Museo Reina Sofia, Madrid.)

Maecenas vehicula, nisl non mattis mattis, purus metus commodo odio, a scelerisque felis leo sed augue. Suspendisse viverra turpis eget lectus placerat, a condimentum risus iaculis. Quisque aliquet est a sem congue venenatis. Vestibulum venenatis aliquet aliquet. Phasellus nec porta leo. Sed sapien sapien, maxim

Morbi est nunc, posuere ut ultricies a, vulputate ac massa. Aenean quis nunc eget lectus placerat tincidunt. Vestibulum ornare, risus eget gravida dictum, diam elit tempus tellus, hendrerit consequat sem purus nec magna. Orci varius natoque penatibus et magnis dis parturient montes, nascetur ridiculus mus. Duis a dictum est.

Example 1. *Concerto No. 1 in E major, Op. 8,* "Spring."

Phasellus sit amet maximus ligula. In tincidunt augue non arcu placerat, a auctor dolor efficitur. Suspendisse lectus odio, commodo quis tellus nec, semper volutpat est. Praesent ut efficitur velit. Aliquam est risus, blandit quis vehicula consequat, commodo id quam. Sed hendrerit pharetra porta. Mauris consectetur, neque id ornare tincidunt, sapien ipsum laoreet sapien, fringilla semper purus libero eu nisl pretium ipsum

23

Tables

Tables are any graphics that use rows and columns to structure the content:
- Follow the same style when presenting tables throughout the paper.

Labels:
- Refer to all tables using label **"table."**

Numbers:
- Number all tables **consequently** throughout the paper:
  - Use **separate numeration** from the illustrations (table 1, table 2, table 3, ...)
- For scientific papers with chapters, use **double numeration**:
  - Each label consists of the chapter number and the table number (table 6.1, table 6.2, table 6.3, ...).
- For tables within appendixes, the number should be preceded by **appendix letters** (A, B, C, ...) and a period:
  - (table A.1, table A.2, table A.3, ...).

Titles:
- The title should summarize the table:
  - Provide titles in **noun form**.
- **Capitalize** the first letter of the title or use **headline-style capitalization**
- Use NO punctuation at the end of the title.

Captions:
- Each caption consists of label, number, and title of table.
- Captions are placed **above** tables.
- Captions are flush left and **single-spaced**.
- Use a period between the number and the title.
- Do not abbreviate the label "table."
- For **long tables** that take several pages, provide a shortened caption on each new page as shown below:
  - Provide column heads on each new page as well:

Example:	Table 1. Number and percentage of students enrolled in DGPI Table 1 (continued)

Callouts:
- In text, provide callouts for each table:
  - Use **spelled-out** and **lowercased** labels with numbers (see table 1, see table 2, see table 3, ...).

Formatting Tables

Keep table structure and filling as simple as possible:
- Spacing and alignment are usually enough to determine the cells:
  - Normally, only 3 horizontal rules are used (after the caption, after the column heads, after the whole table).
- Column heads get sentence-style capitalization:
  - For units of measurement within column heads, include them in parentheses.
- Cells alignment:
  - For short text entries within cells, center the text.
  - For long text entries within cells, flush text to left.
  - For whole numbers within cells, align numbers by the last digit.
  - For fractions with decimal marker, align numbers by the decimal marker:
    - For numbers less than 1.00, omit zero before the decimal marker.
  - If there is no entry to include in cell:
    - Leave the cell empty.
    - Use an em dash (—) for "not applicable."
    - Use three unspaced periods (...) for "no data available."

12

Sed at venenatis massa. Sed vehicula aliquam metus, nec ultrices leo aliquam ut. Morbi turpis sapien, consectetur ut urna vitae, tincidunt volutpat urna. Vivamus justo tellus, semper quis justo sit amet, rutrum accumsan dolor. Curabitur quis neque aliquet, pellentesque erat ac, vulputate velit. Curabitur sit amet dolor sit amet lacus eleifend faucibus id erat.

Table 1. Table title, sentence-style, single-spaced without a period

Stub column head	Spanner head[a]		Spanner head	
	Column head (%)	Column head	Column head (%)	Column head
Stub entry[b]				
Stub subentry	0.00	0.00[*]	0.00	−.82
Stub subentry	...	...	0.00[c]	−.35
Stub entry				
Stub subentry	0.00	0.00[**]	0.00	1.00
Stub subentry	0.00	0.00	0.00	.98
Stub entry	0.00	0.00[*]	0.00[c]	.04

Source: Source note to acknowledge the source of the data.

Note: General note to the whole table.

[a] Specific note to the spanner head.

[b] Specific note to the stub entry.

[c] Specific note to the cell.

* $p < .08$

** $p < .02$

Nunc scelerisque libero at neque ultricies, tempor posuere augue molestie. Suspendisse elementum tincidunt tincidunt. Sed at venenatis massa. Vivamus justo tellus, semper quis justo sit amet, rutrum accumsan dolor. Curabitur quis neque aliquet, pellentesque erat ac, vulputate velit. Curabitur sit amet dolor sit amet lacus eleifend faucibus id a erat. Proin ex mi, aliquet nec ligula ut, dapibus eleifend erat. Proin quis lobortis ex. Nam in pulvinar libero. Proin fermentum ut orci quis sagittis. Donec convallis lectus et tincidunt fringilla.

There are 4 types of notes to the table (arranged in this order):

1. **Source notes**:
   o Source notes are tables' credit lines (acknowledge sources of the table data).
   o Introduce source notes by "*Source:*" or "*Sources:*" (capitalized, italicized, and followed by colon).
2. **General notes**:
   o General notes apply to the whole table.
   o Introduce general notes by "*Note:*" (capitalized, italicized, and followed by colon).
3. **Specific notes**:
   o Specific notes apply to specific parts of tables and appear in the form of:
      ▪ Superscripted letters ([a], [b], [c], …).
      ▪ Superscripted numbers ([1], [2], [3], …).
      ▪ Superscripted symbols (*, †, ‡, §, ‖, #, **, ††, ‡‡, …).
   o Use one system for all tables throughout the paper.
4. **Probability notes** (notes on significance):
   o Use asterisks (*):
      ▪ For several levels of significance, use one asterisk (*) for the least significant level, two asterisks (**) for the next significant level, and so on.
   o Lowercase and italicize probability symbol (p).
   o Omit zero before the decimal marker.

Example:

Sources: Data from Evelyn Henderson, "Effects of Social Networking Sites," *The Washington Post*, January 16, 2020, 12; Thompson, "Writing and Performance," 219; Jameson Gonzales, "Social Networking Sites," speech, University of California, April 16, 2017, San Francisco, radio broadcast, MPEG copy, 1:15:22, https://www.universityofcalifornia.edu/executive/lect/nn=34965872.

Note: Presented value is a mean average.

[a] Refers to the first part of the research.

[b] New results.

* $p < .08$

** $p < .04$

3.8 Text Styling, Punctuation, and Grammar

Italics

- Use italics to **emphasize** words, phrases, etc. sparingly:

Example:	It *is* a problem!

- Use italics to introduce unfamiliar words in **foreign languages** (only on the first mention):

Example:	I wanted to have a *coq au vin* for dinner.

Boldface and Underscore

- As an option, to emphasize words, phrases, etc. use boldface or underscore (underlining):
  - For formal papers, the use of italics is preferred.

Capitalization

Chicago style recommends **minimal** capitalization; therefore, general rules are to capitalize:
- The first letter of the first word of a new sentence (There is…).
- The subject pronoun "I."
- The names and initials of people (I. K. Richardson).
- The names of months (April).
- The days of week (Monday).
- Proper nouns (Saudi Arabia).

Commas

- Use commas for **items in a series**:
  - Use **Oxford comma** (serial comma / series comma) — comma placed before conjunctions "and" and "or" joining last two items in a series of three and more items:

Example:	The color theme is white, pink, and purple.

- Use commas **before "etc."** for items in a series:
  - Do not use commas after "etc." for items in a series:

Example:	The exhibition was beyond any expectations (featuring paintings, sculptures, photographs, etc.).

- Use commas **before conjunctions** "and," "or," "but," "nor," "for," "so," "yet" joining **independent** clauses:
  - Do not use commas if there is only one subject:

Example:	We got to the beach house, and it started raining. We got to the beach house and fell asleep.

- Use commas with **introductory phrases**:

Example:	By 2020, she had opened a restaurant.

- Use commas with **locations** and **dates** in "Month Day, Year" format:

Example:	… London, Great Britain, … … May 22, 2021 …

- Use commas with **titles** that follow the person's name:

Example:	Jane Clark, a senator from Kentucky, visited the museum.

- Do not use commas with "too" at the end of the sentence:
  - Use commas with **"too"** placed in the **middle** of the sentence:

Example:	They decided to go with us too. They, too, decided to go with us.

Quotation Marks with Other Punctuation

- Use single quotation marks (' ') **within** double quotation marks (" "):
  - Use double quotation marks (" ") within single quotation marks (' ') and **so on**:

Example:	Jane said, "I quote, 'Many people who find themselves in "domestic violence" sometimes try to justify the abuser's actions,' meaning that they protect them, blame themselves, or even justify their actions thinking, 'Things would get "better"!' "

- Place periods and commas **before** closing quotation marks:

Example:	Daniel Howard considers them "being intrigued to a particular individual." "A state's development cannot rely on economic status alone," she said.

- Place colons and semicolons **after** closing quotation marks:

Example:	"The Legal Titan and the 'Real Housewife': The Rise and Fall of Tom Girardi and Erika Jayne" I was supposed to write a research on "Agricultural Environment"; instead I was assigned to work on "Agricultural Machinery."

- Place question marks and exclamation points **before or after** closing quotation marks depending on where they belong:

Example:	She asked, "Where do we go?" Where did you find "Grammar Tool"?

Parentheses with Periods

- For **independent sentences** in parentheses, **include** periods in parentheses:
  - Otherwise, do not include periods in parentheses:
    - If the last word in parentheses is "etc." and a period outside parentheses is needed, use both periods:

Example:	The exhibition was beyond any expectations. (It featured paintings, sculptures, and photographs among others.) The exhibition was beyond any expectations (featuring paintings, sculptures, and photographs). The exhibition was beyond any expectations (featuring paintings, sculptures, photographs, etc.).

Passive Voice vs. Active Voice

- Chicago style **prefers** the use of active voice:

Poor:	The poster will be presented by Jeremiah Collins.
Preferable:	Jeremiah Collins will present the poster.

Agreement of Pronouns

- Treat indefinite pronouns "anybody," "somebody," "everybody," "nobody," "anyone," etc. as **singulars**:

Example:	Nobody hears what I say.

- Rewrite the sentences with pronouns joined by "either ... or" and "neither ... nor" to **avoid awkward forms** of verbs:
  - As an option, replace "either ... or" with "one of ... "
  - As an option, replace "neither ... nor" with "neither of ..."

Poor:	Either she or I am crazy. Neither she nor you are crazy.
Preferable:	One of us is crazy. Neither of you is crazy.

3.9 Abbreviations

General Guidelines

Generally, **spell out** an unfamiliar abbreviation **on the first mention**:
- Include the abbreviation in parentheses immediately after:

Example:	According to mean square error (MSE), ...

- Use periods for abbreviations that end with **lowercase letters**:
  - a.m., p.m., e.g., etc., et al., Mr., Dr.
- Use no periods for abbreviations that have two and more **capital letters**:
  - US, CA, CEO, PhD
- Use no periods for abbreviations of **academic degrees**:
  - MA, MS, MD, PhD
- Use periods with spaces for initials in the **person's name** (unless the entire name is written with initials):
  - T. D. F. Thompson, KBH
- Use NO spaces around an **ampersand** (&) for initials in the company's name:
  - D&G, California F&O

Chicago style recommends consulting *Merriam-Webster's Collegiate Dictionary* and *Acronyms, Initialisms & Abbreviations Dictionary* to check spelling of specific abbreviations.

Names and Titles

- Use abbreviations:
  - "Mr.," "Ms.," "Mrs.," "Dr." only **before** full names and surnames.
  - "Rep.," "Sen.," "Adm." only **before full** names.
  - "Rev." and "Hon." only **before full** names.
  - "Jr." and "Sr." only **after full** names.
- Otherwise, spell out the titles.

- Do not use "Ms. President" or "Mrs. President"; instead use "Madam President."

Place Names

Chicago style now allows to use **"US"** both as **noun and adjective**:

Example:	the US US dollars

In the text, always **spell out** the US states and provinces:
- Use commas for states and provinces that follow the names of cities:

Example:	Menlo Park, California, is one of the most educated cities in the United States.

In bibliography/reference list, use standard postal **abbreviations** for the US states and provinces where needed:
- For widely known city (New York, London, etc.), list only the name of the city.
- For little-known city, list the name of the city followed by the US state/province abbreviation or country name:

Example:	New York Menlo Park, CA London Newton Abbot, United Kingdom

Months and Days of the Week

Normally, months and days of the week are **written in full**:
- If the space is limited, use the following abbreviations for formal papers:

Months:		Days of the Week:
Jan.	July	Sun.
Feb.	Aug.	Mon.
Mar.	Sept.	Tues.
Apr.	Oct.	Wed.
May	Nov.	Thurs.
June	Dec.	Fri.
		Sat.

Units of Measurement

	Rule	Example
General	Abbreviations do not change to plural forms	5 gal. 8 m
US Units	For US units of measurement, use periods	in. ft. oz. lb. sq. mi. cu. in.
	As an option, use symbols of inches and feet	5 ft., 3 in. 5'3"
SI Units	For SI base units of measurement, do NOT use periods	m kg K
	Italicize the symbols of SI base units	m, mass l, length t, time

Standard Abbreviations for Citations

Meaning:	Abbreviations:	Meaning:	Abbreviations:
Paragraph	para.	Appendix	app.
Part	pt.	Supplement	suppl.
Article	art.	Edition	ed.
Section	sec.	Editor	ed.
Chapter	chap.	Editors	eds.
Series	ser.	Translator, Translators	trans.
Division	div.	Revised	rev.
Volume	vol.	Manuscript	MS
Number	no.	No date	n.d.
Numbers	nos.	And others	et al.

3.10 Bias-Free and Inclusive Language

To bring writing in line with best modern practices, Chicago style encourages to be **respectful** to sensitive individuals and group identities by avoiding biases and choosing inclusive language:
- Focus on the paper's ideas instead of political subtext.
- Avoid offensive language.

Gender Bias

Chicago recommends **AVOIDING** the following techniques when referring to no one particularly:
- Usage of generic masculine pronoun "he."
- Usage of generic pronoun "he/she" or "s/he."
- Usage of pronoun "they" as singular.

Chicago style recommends **rewriting** the text if possible.

Alternatively, when referring to no one particular, always use pronouns "they," "them," "their," "themselves" as **plurals**:
- Use pronouns "they," "them," "their," "themselves" to refer to **one person** as well:

Example:	The editor-in-chief will interview the senator themselves.

Gender-Neutral Language

Avoid word choices that imply that only one sex is the norm:
- Use words **"people"** instead of "men" or "women":
  - However, some writing may refer to only one sex (for example, topics on pregnancy); in this case use gender-specific terms to **avoid absurd**.
- Avoid using words with **masculine suffixes** "-man" or **feminine suffixes** "-ess" and "-ette":

Sexist Terms:	Alternative Gender-Neutral Terms:
policeman	police officer
fireman	firefighter
spokesman	representative

Other Biases and Inclusive Language

Use inclusive language and avoid biases in regards to age, gender, sexual orientations, race, ethnicity, religion, social status:
- Remain **accurate** when using labels.
- Avoid using pronouns that **exclude** or generalize.
- Use **descriptive** phrases to label a group of people instead of using adjectives as nouns.
- Use **exact** age ranges instead of broad categories, etc.

Exclusive Language:	Preferred:
the Muslims	Shia Muslims
We are all concerned about what is happening.	Most people are concerned about what is happening.
the blind	people who are blind

4.0 REFERENCING

4.1 General Guidelines

Referencing **allows writers** to avoid accusations of plagiarism and academic dishonesty in their works.

Referencing **acknowledges** the sources used in papers:
1. In the text, use in-text citations to mark the cited material and name sources.
2. At the end of paper, include a list of all sources referred to in paper.

Referencing **allows readers** to follow any in-text citation to find the source listed at the end of paper and vice versa.

What Requires Citations

Providing opinions / ideas / theories / facts / statistics found in someone else's requires citation in the form of:
1. **Paraphrase** – restating specific ideas from another work **in your own words**.
2. **Summary** – providing **general idea** from another work.
3. **Quotation** or direct quote – **exact reproduction** of original material from another work using the same language:
   - Quotations are normally enclosed in double quotation marks.

What Does NOT Require Citations

Do not cite the following:
- Commonly known facts (common knowledge, biographical facts about famous people, historical events, etc.).
- Proverbs and other familiar expressions.
- Your own opinion.

Signal Phrases

Signal phrases (attributive tags / narrative citation) are used in the text to signal that the material is from an outside source:
- Signal phrases usually consist of the author's name and a respective verb.
- Signal phrases usually appear directly before or right after the citation:

Example:	Meryl Adams highlights, "The normal functioning of organs like the liver and kidney are adversely affected by alcohol consumption in excess."

Steps to Referencing

Step 1

Record:
- Write down all publication information about the sources necessary for citations:
  - **Authors** and other contributors (editors, translators, illustrators, creators, directors, etc.).
  - **Titles**, subtitles, chapter/article titles, periodical titles; series, volumes, issues, editions, page numbers, etc.
  - **Publishers**, place of publication, year of publication, databases, DOIs/URLs, access dates, etc.

Step 2

Organize:
- Store the sources in format that is easy to access at any time.
- As an option, use "EndNote" software to manage references and format citations correctly.

Step 3

Cite:
- Include citations in the text using appropriate guidelines.

Step 4

List:
- Create bibliography/reference list at the end of your paper.

4.2 Two Referencing Systems (NB and AD)

Chicago style uses **two referencing systems**:
1. Notes and Bibliography (NB) referencing system.
2. Author-Date (AD) referencing system.

Two systems are **identical in content**, but are different in form:

Notes and Bibliography **(NB)** Referencing System	Author-Date **(AD)** Referencing System
• Notes and Bibliography (NB) referencing system uses numbered notes in the text to direct the reader to footnotes (citations at the bottom of the page) or endnotes (citations at the end of the paper). • Each note (footnote or endnote) links to the full entry on the bibliography page at the end of the paper.	• Author-Date (AD) referencing system uses parenthetical citations in the text to reference the source (author and the year of publication). • Each parenthetical citation links to the full entry on a references page at the end of the paper.

There are two parts to referencing for each system:
1. **In-text citations** within the text of paper:
    • NB system uses notes (footnotes or endnotes).
    • AD system uses parenthetical citations.
2. **List of sources** at the end of paper:
    • NB system uses bibliography.
    • AD system uses reference list.

Parts of Referencing / System	Notes and Bibliography **(NB)** Referencing System	Author-Date **(AD)** Referencing System
1. Citation within the Text	Notes (Footnotes/Endnotes)	Parenthetical Citations
2. List of Sources	Bibliography	References

Reference list entries are formatted like the bibliography entries with the **only difference**:
• The date of publication follows the author's name:

Example:		
Parts of Referencing / System	Notes and Bibliography **(NB)** Referencing System	Author-Date **(AD)** Referencing System
1. Citations within the Text	There is a huge influence of the environment in shaping people's behavior, personality, and perception.[1] --- 1. James Brooks, Favorite Athlete (New York: Pocket Books, 2018), 43.	There is a huge influence of the environment in shaping people's behavior, personality, and perception (Brooks 2018, 43).
2. List of Sources	Bibliography Brooks, James. Favorite Athlete. New York: Pocket Books, 2018.	References Brooks, James. 2018. Favorite Athlete. New York: Pocket Books.

Consult your instructor for the preferred referencing system.

4.3 Titles of Works

The following guidelines refer to the titles of works mentioned in the text, notes (footnotes/endnotes), and bibliography/reference list:

- Titles get **headline-style capitalization** (except titles in languages other than English):

DO CAPITALIZE	Don't capitalize
<ul><li>Nouns</li><li>Pronouns</li><li>Verbs</li><li>Adjectives</li><li>Adverbs</li><li>Subordinating conjunctions:<ul><li>That</li><li>If</li><li>As If</li><li>As Soon As</li><li>Although</li><li>Because</li><li>Unless</li><li>Till</li><li>Until</li><li>How</li><li>When</li><li>Where</li><li>While</li><li>Who</li><li>Why</li><li>Before</li><li>After</li></ul></li></ul>	<ul><li>Articles:<ul><li>a</li><li>an</li><li>the</li></ul></li><li>Coordinating conjunctions:<ul><li>and</li><li>or</li><li>but</li><li>nor</li><li>yet</li><li>for</li><li>so</li></ul></li><li>Prepositions:<ul><li>between</li><li>against</li><li>according to</li><li>to</li><li>in</li><li>at</li><li>on</li><li>of</li><li>as</li></ul></li><li>The infinitive "to"</li></ul>

- Separate title and **subtitle** with a colon:
  - The first word of title and subtitle is always capitalized:

Example:	Exploring the Role of Warrior as an Aspect of Peace Studies
	Causes and Effects: The Popularity of Fast Food Restaurants

- **Styling** of titles depends on the **type of work**:

Italicized	**"In Double Quotation Marks"**	**Not Formatted**
Titles of larger works (full volumes) are italicized:<ul><li>*Books*</li><li>*Periodicals:*<ul><li>*Journals*</li><li>*Newspapers*</li><li>*Magazines*</li></ul></li><li>*Plays*</li><li>*Very Long Poems*</li><li>*Videos*</li><li>*Compact Discs*</li><li>*Movies, TV shows*</li><li>*Cartoons*</li><li>*Podcast Series*</li><li>*Video Games*</li><li>*Paintings, Photographs*</li><li>*Official Maps*</li><li>*Small Exhibitions*</li></ul>	Titles of shorter works (items within full volumes) are enclosed in double quotation marks:<ul><li>"Chapters"</li><li>"Articles"</li><li>"Smaller Poems and Rhymes"</li><li>"Songs"</li><li>"Videos"</li><li>"Scenes"</li><li>"Episodes"</li><li>"Fairy Tales"</li><li>"Short Stories"</li><li>"Dissertations"</li><li>"Lectures"</li></ul>	Titles that are neither italicized nor enclosed in double quotation marks:<ul><li>Websites (Wikipedia)</li><li>Trademarked Games (Twister)</li><li>Ancient Artworks with Unknown Creators (Medici Venus)</li><li>Large Exhibitions (World's Columbian Exposition)</li><li>Applications, Devices, Operations Systems (Windows, iOS, Kindle, Firefox)</li></ul>

Example:	My favorite book is *Harry Potter and the Sorcerer's Stone.* Have you read the *Los Angeles Times* article "The Legal Titan and the 'Real Housewife'"? I did not use Wikipedia for my research.

- Titles of works included in other titles of works are always styled as guided by Chicago style:

Example: (title of the article about book)	"Kennedy Price's *New World:* Full Review of the Book"

- Titles of works included in paper's headings are also styled as guided by Chicago style:

Example: (Heading in the paper)	**Problems of Kennedy Price's *New World***

Changes to Titles

Reproduce the title of works **in full exactly** as they appear in the original source in terms of spelling and punctuation, but:
- Change original title capitalization to **headline-style capitalization**.
- Always use a **colon to separate title and subtitle** (even if original title contains another punctuation or no punctuation at all):
  - The first word of title and subtitle is always capitalized.
- Add a comma according to grammar if it was omitted from the original title for aesthetic reasons.
- As an option, replace an ampersand (&) with "and."

- For **double titles** connected by "or" (alternative titles), use the original source's punctuation:
  - Use a comma if the original source does not contain punctuation.
  - Always capitalize the first letter of the second title:

Example:	*Communication Skills, or Adventure in Building Communication with Children*

- **In text,** for mentions of **periodical titles**, the initial article "the" is lowercased and is not italicized (even if it is a part of the original periodical title):

Example:	I always read the *Wall Street Journal,* but my wife prefers the *New York Times.*

Shortening Titles

For the first mention of the title of work in the text, use the full title:
- For **subsequent mentions** of titles in the text, use shortened forms of titles.

Shorten the title only if it has more than four words:
- Include **up to four "keywords"** from the full title:
  - **Omit** the initial article **"A," "An," "The."**
- Do not change the order of the words.
- Do not paraphrase the title.
- Do not change styling of the title:

Full Title Example	Shortened Title Example
In the Time of Medicine and Anatomy Research	*Medicine and Anatomy Research*
"The Live Art: Awakened Performer"	"Live Art"
"'The Boar Year' and Jackie Robinson"	"'Boar Year'"
"Kennedy Price's *New World:* Full Review of the Book"	"Price's *New World*"

4.4 Quotations

Quotation (quote) is the **exact reproduction** of original material from another work:
- Do not change spelling, punctuation, order of the words, etc. when using quotations in the paper.

Remember to place the superscripted number (NB) or use a parenthetical quotation (AD) at the end of the quotation:

Notes and Bibliography **(NB)** Referencing System	Author-Date **(AD)** Referencing System
Meryl Adams highlights, "The normal functioning of organs like the liver and kidney are adversely affected by alcohol consumption in excess."[1]	Meryl Adams highlights, "The normal functioning of organs like the liver and kidney are adversely affected by alcohol consumption in excess" (Sebastian 2015, 47).

There are two types of quotations to present in the text:
1. **Short quotations:**
   - Take less than 100 words.
   - Are integrated into the main text.
2. **Long quotations:**
   - Take more than 100 words.
   - Are set off from the main text as indented blocks.

Short Quotations (Run-In Quotations)

Short quotations (run-in quotations) take **less than 100 words** (approximately, 5 lines of text):
- Integrate short quotations in the main text.
- Enclose short quotations in **double quotation marks**:

Example:	Meryl Adams highlights, "The normal functioning of organs like the liver and kidney are adversely affected by alcohol consumption in excess."

Long Quotations (Block Quotes / Extras)

Long quotations (block quotes / extras) take **more than 100 words** (approximately, 5 lines of text):
- **Set off** long quotations from the main text as blocks:
  - Indent the whole block **0.5 inches** from the left:
    - Alternatively, use smaller font to set off the block.
  - Do not indent any lines inside the block.
  - Leave **one empty line** before and after the block.
- Do not enclose block quotes in double quotation marks.
- Block quotes are **single-spaced**.
- Block quotes are usually introduced by a colon.

Example:	Companies scrutinize their business models, break new ground proactively, and develop new skills:
	It is to be expected that digitalization due to performance increase and simultaneous cost reduction will capture all parts of the economy and society. Depending on the point of view digitalization is explained with actual trends which influence patterns of behavior of customers, value-added structures, and the working life. Digitalization is also associated with the challenges and changes that come along for companies.

Poetry

- **Generally**, poetry quotations are set off as **block quotes**:
  - Indent runover lines one em dash (—) from the left:

Example:	Even so my sun one early morn did shine
	With all-triumphant splendour
	   on my brow;
	But out, alack! he was but one hour mine;
	The region cloud hath mask'd him
	   from me now.
	Yet him for this my love no whit disdaineth;
	Suns of the world may stain when
	   heaven's sun staineth.

- For a **short** (1–2 lines) **poetry quotation**, integrate it in the text:
  - Mark a break at the end of each line, use a slash with space before and after (/).
  - Mark a stanza break, use two slashes with space before and after (//):

Example:	Emily Gallacher writes, "Fifth, become a respected attending in intensive care / Bark orders at residents, rest easy in your big house."

Dialogue

- Enclose dialogue replicas in **double quotation marks**:
  - Use a new line to mark another speaker's replica:

Example:	"Thank you so much. I don't know how to repay you for this. I think she was going to kill me." "That's the easy way out. I think you should have to live and suffer for what you've done." "I'll give you anything. Please just let me go."

Drama

- For play quotations:
  - **Do not set off or enclose in double quotation marks**.
  - Identify each speaker by the respective label:
    - Write the label in **all capital letters**.
    - Follow the label with a period.
  - Provide an additional hanging indent for all subsequent lines of each replica.
  - Italicize stage directions:

Example:	FORD. I warrant. What, Robin, I say! (*Enter Servants with a basket.*) PAGE. Come, come, come. FORD. Here, set it down. FALSTAFF, *coming forward.* Let me see it, let me see it! Follow your friend's counsel.

Introducing Quotations and Punctuation

Quotation Marks

- Quotations in the text are enclosed in double quotation marks:
  - **Quotations within quotations** are also enclosed in quotation marks; however:
    - Use single quotation marks (') within double quotation marks (" ").
    - Use double quotation marks (" ") within single quotation marks (') and so on:

Example:	Jane said, "I quote, 'Many people who find themselves in "domestic violence" sometimes try to justify the abuser's actions,' meaning that they protect them, blame themselves, or even justify their actions thinking, 'Things would get "better"!' "

Comma Before

- **Generally,** use a comma to **introduce run-in quotations** (usually after words "said," "found," and the like):
  - o Capitalize the first letter of run-in quotations:

Example:	Young writes, "It was necessary for America to build more ships for their merchants."

Colon Before

- Use a colon to **formally introduce run-in quotations** (usually after introductory phrase "as follows" and the like):
  - o Capitalize the first letter of run-in quotations:

Example:	Young has a strong opinion as follows: "It was necessary for America to build more ships."

- Use a colon to **introduce block quotes**:
  - o Capitalize the first letter of block quotes:

Example:	Companies scrutinize their business models, break new ground proactively, and develop new skills:
	It is to be expected that digitalization due to performance increase and simultaneous cost reduction will capture all parts of the economy and society. ...

Period Before

- As an option, precede block quotes by a period:
  - o Note that such a technique should be used **consistently** throughout the paper:

Example:	Companies scrutinize their business models, break new ground proactively, and develop new skills.
	It is to be expected that digitalization due to performance increase and simultaneous cost reduction will capture all parts of the economy and society. Depending on the point of view digitalization is explained with actual trends which influence patterns of behavior of customers, value-added structures, and the working life. Digitalization is also associated with the challenges and changes that come along for companies.

No Punctuation Before

- Do not use any punctuation to introduce quotations that are **syntactical parts** of surrounding text:
  - o Lowercase the first letter of quotations in this case:

Example:	As Rodriguez argues, it was a reflection that "the nature of people was in a position to push development in the country a notch higher."
	Daniel Howard considers them "intrigued to a particular individual for a minute."

Example:	Companies scrutinize their business models, break new ground proactively, and develop new skills because
	it is to be expected that digitalization due to performance increase and simultaneous cost reduction will capture all parts of the economy and society. Depending on the point of view digitalization is explained with actual trends which influence patterns of behavior of customers, on value-added structures, and the working life. Digitalization is also associated with the challenges and changes that come along for companies.

Comma After

- Use a comma at the end of run-in quotations when the sentence is **inverted** (signal phrase appears after quotation):

Example:	"A state's development cannot rely on economic status alone," Allan Anderson noted.

Two Commas

- Use two commas to **interrupt** run-in quotations:

Example:	"I believe," Emily cried, "that is him!"

Text Following Block Quote

- Generally, **indent** the text following block quote as a new paragraph:
  - Do not indent the text following block quote if it is a continuation of the paragraph that introduces the block quote.

Making Changes to Quotations

Permissible Changes

Quotations should be reproduced exactly in terms of spelling, punctuation, order of the words, etc.:
- However, to **assimilate quotation** into typography of the paper, the following changes are permitted:
  1. Double quotation marks may be changed to single quotation marks and vice versa.
  2. All-capital letters may be changed to small letters.
  3. Underlined words may be changed to italicized words.

As long as the meaning of the quotations remains the same, the **writer may**:
- Shorten quotations (omit parts of quotations).
- Clarify quotations.
- Highlight mistakes in quotations.
- Add emphasis to quotations

Omitting Parts of Quotations

Whenever you omit words, phrases, or sentences, make sure it would not confuse or cause misunderstanding for readers:
- Use **ellipsis — three spaced periods** (. . .) — to indicate that some part of the quotation has been left out.
- Do not use ellipses at the beginning or at the end of quotation:

Example:	According to Adam Reed and Victor Hernandez, "Other than making sure the economic interactions in the region are active and peaceful . . . the Silk Road will also act as an economic and infrastructure incentive."

- As an option, put ellipses in **square brackets** ([. . .]) for **aesthetic** reasons:

Example:	"It is to be expected that digitalization due to performance increase and simultaneous cost reduction will capture all parts of the economy and society [. . .]. Digitalization is also associated with the challenges and changes that come along for companies."

- To mark the omission of one or several lines in the poetry, use **a line of spaced periods** (. . . . .) approximately the length of an average line:

Example:	Alfred Tennyson's "Tears, Idle Tears" is a great example:
	Ah, sad and strange as in dark summer dawns
	. . . .
	The casement slowly grows a glimmering square;
	So sad, so strange, the days that are no more.

Clarifying Quotations

- To clarify, explain, or comment, use **square brackets** ([]):

Example:	"Mitchell B[rakman] was absent during the voting."

- To **include missing words** in quotation, use square brackets ([]):
  o Use a question mark for uncertainty:

Example:	In the view of Patterson, "the [election?] results are in sync with states' presidential votes."

Highlighting Mistakes

- To highlight a spelling or grammatical mistake made in an original source rather than in the paper, use [*sic*] (from Latin "thus" or "so") directly after the mistake:
  o **Italicize "sic" and put it in square brackets**:

Example:	In the view of Jenkins, "Impaired judgment, nausea, laziness and impractical crave for food leads [*sic*] to general body malfunctions."

Adding Emphasis

- For rare cases when attention to specific words is needed, **italicize** them to add emphasis:
  o In NB referencing system, include "italics mine" or "italics added" in the note.
  o In AD referencing system, include "italics mine" or "italics added" in the parenthetical citation:

Example:	Notes and Bibliography **(NB)** Referencing System	Author-Date **(AD)** Referencing System
	2. Morgan, "Five Things," 75; italics added.	... (Morgan 1994, 75; italics added).

- To mark the words that are emphasized in original source, **italicize** them and **add** "italics in the original" in **square brackets** directly after italics:

Example:	According to Brooks, "the results reflected *local* [italics in the original] patterns."

4.5 In-Text Citations

4.5.1 NB System: Notes (Footnotes/Endnotes)

Within NB referencing system, in-text citations appear in **form of notes**:
1. Footnotes (placed at the bottom of the page),
2. Endnotes (placed at the end of the paper).

To cite a source in text:
1. Use a **superscripted number** in the text placed after the cited material (quote, summary, or paraphrase).
2. Use a **respective numbered note** to include the full information about the source.

Example:	
	There is a huge influence of the environment in shaping people's behavior, personality, and perception.[1] _____
	1. James Brooks, Favorite Athlete (New York: Pocket Books, 2018), 43.

- In the text:
  - o Note numbers are **superscripted**.
- In the notes (footnotes/endnotes):
  - o Note numbers are **full-sized** followed by period and space.

Notes Formatting

General guidelines:
- Notes may contain citations, comments, or both.
- Notes are set smaller than the main text of paper.
- Notes are **single-spaced**.
- Notes elements are separated with commas and end with period.
- Leave **one empty line** between notes.
- Note numbers start with 1 and follow throughout a paper:
  - o Note numbers are superscripted in the text and are full-sized within notes section:
    - Each superscripted number corresponds to note.
    - List notes in the same order as they appear in the text.
- The first line of note is indented 0.5 inches:
  - o Subsequent lines are flush left.
- Always use a new note number for each new citation in text.
- Do not use several note numbers at the end of a single citation:
  - o Instead, use one note number at the of a citation and include several sources within a single note.

Each type of source has specific format for notes:
- Check chapter "NB SYSTEM: NOTES / BIBLIOGRAPHY EXAMPLES" of this guide for detailed formatting guidelines.

Full Notes

Include complete information about the source only the **first time it is cited**:
1. Author (full name),
2. Title (full title),
3. Publication information, etc.

Check chapter "NB SYSTEM: NOTES / BIBLIOGRAPHY EXAMPLES" of this guide for more information.

Example:	1. Mason White, "Nonviolence in Action," *Peace Studies*, March 2020, 49. 2. Olivia Smith, *The Nicest Place We Would Need to Go* (New York: Aspen, 2019), 34.

Shortened Notes

Whenever citing the source again, use shortened notes for subsequent citations:
- Shortened notes include:
  - Author (only last name),
  - Title (shortened title up to four words),
  - Page number or another locator.

Example:	1. Olivia Smith, *The Nicest Place We Would Need to Go* (New York: Aspen, 2019), 34. 2. … 3. … 4. Smith, *Nicest Place*, 39.

Ibid.

When citing the **same source that has just been cited**, use the abbreviation "Ibid." (from Latin "in the same place"):
- "Ibid." means that the citation refers to the same source cited above (in the preceding note).
- Additionally, include the page number if it is different from the above (preceding) note:

Example:	1. Mason White, "Nonviolence in Action," *Peace Studies*, March 2020, 49. 2. Olivia Smith, *The Nicest Place We Would Need to Go* (New York: Aspen, 2019), 34. 3. Ibid. 4. Ibid., 36. 5. White, "Nonviolence in Action," 49. 6. Ibid., 51. 7. Ibid. 8. Ibid., 49–50.

"Ibid." vs. Shortened Citations

Chicago style **discourages** the use of "Ibid.":
- Instead, use shortened notes:
  - Title of work can be omitted in this case.
- Include the page number even if it is same as the above (preceding) note:

Example:	1. Mason White, "Nonviolence in Action," *Peace Studies*, March 2020, 49. 2. Olivia Smith, *The Nicest Place We Would Need to Go* (New York: Aspen, 2019), 34. 3. Smith, 34. 4. Smith, 36. 5. White, "Nonviolence in Action," 49. 6. White, 51. 7. White, 51. 8. White, 49–50.

- Footnotes are placed at the **bottom of the page** (footer):
    o As an option, separate footnotes from the main text with a **short line**.
- Each footnote is placed on the same page where the superscripted number appears:

Example:

12

      Pellentesque habitant urna eget mi pharetra, eget luctus elit cursus. Phasellus facilisis quam dapibus odio iaculis pulvinar.[1] Pellentesque nec mollis urna. Sed a tempus enim. Vestibulum vitae odio hendrerit, dictum ipsum id, auctor mauris. Donec lobortis leo mi, quis pharetra tortor viverra sed. Donec interdum auctor condimentum.[2]

      Cras metus nulla, commodo vel lacus quis, imperdiet vehicula sapien. Orci varius natoque penatibus et magnis dis parturient montes, nascetur ridiculus mus. Ut id nisi commodo, elementum nibh in, mattis nunc.[3] Etiam auctor lobortis sem eu lacinia. In hac habitasse platea dictumst. Nulla justo arcu, scelerisque eu ornare sed, vehicula a arcu.[4]

---

1. Mason White, "Nonviolence in Action," *Peace Studies*, March 2020, 49.

2. Olivia Smith, *The Nicest Place We Would Need to Go* (New York: Aspen, 2019), 34.

3. White, "Nonviolence in Action," 49.

4. White, 50.

Endnotes

- Endnotes are placed at the **end of the paper** on a **separate page**:
    o Endnotes follow the main body pages and appendixes.
    o Endnotes precede bibliography.
- Title the page "Notes" (centered at the top with no additional styling).
- Endnotes are set smaller than the main text but larger than footnotes.
- If the paper is divided into chapters, additionally use chapter titles to separate notes:

Example:

33

Notes

1. Mason White, "Nonviolence in Action," *Peace Studies*, March 2020, 49.

2. Olivia Smith, *The Nicest Place We Would Need to Go* (New York: Aspen, 2019), 34.

3. White, "Nonviolence in Action," 49.

4. White, 50.

To insert a footnote / endnote in Microsoft Word:

1. Place cursor in text where a superscripted number should appear.
2. Select "References."
3. Select "Insert Footnote" / "Insert Endnote."

    A superscripted number will be inserted in text and the corresponding number will be placed at the bottom of the page (footer) / at the end of the document.

1 Author

- For the source with 1 author, include the author's full name in full note and only last name in shortened note:

	General Format	Example
Note	#. Firstname Lastname, …	1. Olivia Smith, …
Shortened Note	#. Lastname, …	2. Smith, …

2 Authors

- For the source with 2 authors, include the authors' full names in full note and only last names in shortened note:

	General Format	Example
Note	#. Firstname Lastname and Firstname Lastname, …	1. Liam Scott and Zoey Torres, …
Shortened Note	#. Lastname and Lastname, …	2. Scott and Torres, …

3 Authors

- For the source with 3 authors, include the authors' full names in full note and only last names in shortened note:
  - Separate names with comma.
  - Use an Oxford comma before the final "and":

	General Format	Example
Note	#. Firstname Lastname, Firstname Lastname, and Firstname Lastname, …	1. Julian Johnson, Caroline Green, and Aaron Peterson, …
Shortened Note	#. Lastname, Lastname, and Lastname, …	2. Johnson, Green, and Peterson, …

4+ Authors

- For the source with 4+ authors, include only the first author's full name **followed by "et al."** in full note and only last name **followed by "et al."** in shortened note:

	General Format	Example
Note	#. Firstname Lastname et al., …	1. Noah Williams et al., …
Shortened Note	#. Lastname et al., …	2. Williams et al., …

Organization as Author

- For the source with an organization as author, use organization name instead of the author's name:

	General Format	Example
Note	#. Organization, …	1. World Medical Relief, …
Shortened Note	#. Organization, …	2. World Medical Relief, …

No Author

- For the source with no author, omit the author from the entry and **begin with the following element** (title of work):
  - Alternatively use "Anonymous" in the place of author:

	General Format	Example
Note	Omit the author or #. Anonymous. …	1. *How to Eradicate Corruption* (Munich: K. G. Saur, 2005), 56. 1. Anonymous. *How to Eradicate Corruption* (Munich: K. G. Saur, 2005), 56.
Shortened Note	Omit the author or #. Anonymous. …	2. *How to Eradicate Corruption*, 58. 2. Anonymous. *How to Eradicate Corruption*, 58.

Locators

For sources with no pages or no fixed pages (e-books, online books, etc.), include **any other locator** (section heading, chapter title, paragraph, etc.) instead of the page number:

- For small searchable documents, locators may be omitted:

Locator	Example
Page	1. Miller, *Demonetization*, 48.
Page range	1. Miller, *Demonetization*, 234–45.
Several pages	1. Miller, *Demonetization*, 48, 234–45.
Section	1. Miller, *Demonetization*, sec. 15.
Paragraph	1. Miller, *Demonetization*, § 8.
Equation	1. Miller, *Demonetization*, eq. 19.
Chapter	1. Miller, *Demonetization*, chap. 3.
Volume	1. Miller, *Demonetization*, vol. 5.
Volume and page	1. Miller, *Demonetization*, 5:277.
Note	1. Miller, *Demonetization*, 34n6.
Table	1. Miller, *Demonetization*, table 2.9.
Illustration	1. Miller, *Demonetization*, illus. 6.7.
Other specific location for work with no numerical signposts (electronic source)	1. Miller, *Demonetization*, under "Stripping a Currency Unit."

Additional Information

- To include additional material / commentary / explanation in a note, use a **period** after the note:

General Format:	#. Note. Additional information.
Example:	1. Santiago Evans, "A Railway Accident," This Week, *Transportation Technologies* (Haven, CT), May 14, 2018, Haven edition, sec. D. Evans notes that after the civil war, there was a need for establishing America's presence overseas.

Special Circumstances

2+ Sources within the Same Citation

- To include 2+ sources in a single citation, use **semicolons** to separate notes:
  - If any source has been cited before, use a shortened note:

General Format:	#. Note; Note; … ; Note.
Example:	1. Charlotte Carter, *Encountering Distant Voices: Exploring the Role of Warrior as an Aspect of Peace Studies*, 4th ed., trans. Oliver Stewart (New York: Aspen, 2009), 59, NetLibrary; Brooks, *Favorite Athlete*, 64; Mason White, "Nonviolence in Action," *Peace Studies*, March 2020, 49.

Secondary Sources

Chicago discourages citing sources from secondary sources:
- Try to find the original source to examine it thoroughly.
- If the original source is not available, cite both secondary and original sources:
  - Include full notes for both sources linked by "cited in" or "quoted in":

General Format:	#. Note, cited in / quoted in Note.
Example:	1. Leo Collins, "The Dance of Healing," in *Religion and Psychology*, ed. Cameron Turner (Boston: D. R. Godine, 2006), 319, cited in Evelyn Henderson, "Effects of Social Networking Sites," *The Washington Post*, January 16, 2020, 12.

Place superscripted note number at the end of the citation:
- After all punctuation except dash (comma, period, exclamation point, question mark, colon, semicolon, quotations marks, parentheses, etc.) with no space before:

Example:	After the civil war, there was a need for establishing America's presence overseas, and as such, it was necessary to build bases in other regions.[1]
	However, opponents of imperialism argue that "it goes against America's principles of freedom since imperialism entailed conquering and submission of people against their will."[2]
	Many people who find themselves in domestic violence sometimes try to justify the abuser's actions[3] — they might protect them, blame themselves, or even justify their actions thinking that things would get better.

Summary

		General Format	**Example**
1 Author	**Note**	#. Firstname Lastname, ...	1. Olivia Smith, ...
	Shortened Note	#. Lastname, ...	2. Smith, ...
2 Authors	**Note**	#. Firstname Lastname and Firstname Lastname, ...	1. Liam Scott and Zoey Torres, ...
	Shortened Note	#. Lastname and Lastname, ...	2. Scott and Torres, ...
3 Authors	**Note**	#. Firstname Lastname, Firstname Lastname, and Firstname Lastname, ...	1. Julian Johnson, Caroline Green, and Aaron Peterson, ...
	Shortened Note	#. Lastname, Lastname, and Lastname, ...	2. Johnson, Green, and Peterson, ...
4+ Authors	**Note**	#. Firstname Lastname et al., ...	1. Noah Williams et al., ...
	Shortened Note	#. Lastname et al., ...	2. Williams et al., ...
Organization as Author	**Note**	#. Organization, ...	1. World Medical Relief, ...
	Shortened Note	#. Organization, ...	2. World Medical Relief, ...
No Author	**Note**	Omit the author or #. Anonymous. ...	1. *How to Eradicate Corruption* (Munich: K. G. Saur, 2005), 56. 1. Anonymous. *How to Eradicate Corruption* (Munich: K. G. Saur, 2005), 56.
	Shortened Note	Omit the author or #. Anonymous. ...	2. *How to Eradicate Corruption*, 58. 2. Anonymous. *How to Eradicate Corruption*, 58.
Additional Information	**Note**	#. Note. Additional information.	1. ... . Author notes that there was a need for establishing presence.
	Shortened Note	#. Shortened Note. Additional information.	2. ... . Author notes that there was a need for establishing presence.
2+ Sources within the Same Citation	**Note**	#. Note; Note; ... ; Note.	1. ... ; ... ; ...
	Shortened Note	#. Shortened Note; Shortened Note; ... ; Shortened Note.	2. ... ; ... ; ...
Secondary Sources	**Note**	#. Note, cited in/quoted in Note.	1. ... , cited in ...
	Shortened Note	#. Shortened Note, cited in/quoted in Shortened Note.	2. ... , cited in ...

4.5.2 AD System: Parenthetical Citations

Within AD referencing system, in-text citations appear in parentheses and include **two required elements** with no punctuation:
1. Author(s).
2. Date of publication.

General Format:	... (Author Date)
Example:	... (Scott 2021)

Extended citation **can also include**:
- Page number / any other locator (separated with a comma).
- Any additional information (separated with a semicolon):

General Format:	... (Author Date, locator; additional information)
Example:	... (Scott 2021, 76; the interviewee wished to remain anonymous)

Authors

1 Author

- For the source with 1 author, include the author's last name:

General Format:	... (Lastname Date)
Example:	... (Scott 2021)

2 Authors

- For the source with 2 authors, include both authors' last names with "and":

General Format:	... (Lastname and Lastname Date)
Example:	... (Torres and Williams 2018)

3 Authors

- For the source with 3 authors, include all authors' last names separated with commas:
  - Use an Oxford comma before the final "and":

General Format:	... (Lastname, Lastname, and Lastname Date)
Example:	... (Johnson, Adams, and Gray 2019)

4+ Authors

- For the source with 4+ authors, include only the first author's last name **followed by "et al.":**

General Format:	... (Lastname et al. Date)
Example:	... (Green et al. 2020)

No Author

- For the source with no author, use the shortened title of work in the place of author:
  - Style the title depending on the type of the work (check the chapter "4.3 Titles of Works" for more details):

General Format:	... (*Shortened Title* Date) or ... ("Shortened Title" Date)
Example:	... (*Annoying Commercials* 2016) or ... ("Importance of Family" 2020)

Date

- For the sources with no date of publication, use the abbreviation "n.d." preceded by comma.
- If the date of publication is known for sure but is not provided within the source, include it in square brackets:
  - o If the date of publication is not known for sure or is guessed, include it in square brackets with a questions mark:

General Format:	... (Lastname [Date?]) or ... (Lastname, n.d.)
Example:	... (Murphy [1965?]) or ... (Murphy, n.d.)

Locators

Locators are optional elements of in-text citations; however, it is always **useful to add the page** number to help readers locate the cited material:

- For sources with no pages or no fixed pages (e-books, online books, etc.), include any other locator (section heading, chapter title, paragraph, etc.) instead of the page number.
- To include the page number / any other locator in a citation, use a comma.
- For small searchable documents, locators may be omitted:

General Format:	... (Lastname Date, locator)

Locator	Example
Page	(Miller 2015, 48)
Page range	(Miller 2015, 234–45)
Several pages	(Miller 2015, 48, 234–45)
Section	(Miller 2015, sec. 15)
Paragraph	(Miller 2015, § 8)
Equation	(Miller 2015, eq. 19)
Chapter	(Miller 2015, chap. 3)
Volume	(Miller 2015, vol. 5)
Volume and page	(Miller 2015, 5:277)
Note	(Miller 2015, 34n6)
Table	(Miller 2015, table 2.9)
Illustration	(Miller 2015, illus. 6.7)
Other specific location for work with no numerical signposts (electronic source)	(Miller 2015, under "Stripping a Currency Unit")

Additional Information

- To include additional material / commentary / explanation in a citation, use a **semicolon**:

General Format:	... (Lastname Date, locator; additional information)
Example:	... (Adams 2004, 159; the interviewee wished to remain anonymous)

Special Circumstances

2+ Sources within the Same Citation

- To include 2+ sources within a single citation, use a **semicolon**:

General Format:	... (Lastname Date, locator; Lastname Date, locator; ... ; Lastname Date, locator)
Example:	... (Johnson, Adams, and Gray 2019, 298; Miller 2015, 48)

Citations with the same author and same date must distinguish:

- For different sources with the same author(s) and the same date:
  - o **Assign letters** (a, b, c, …) to the dates to distinguish between the sources:

General Format:	… (Lastname Datea) … (Lastname Dateb)
Example:	… (Watson 2010a) … (Watson 2010b)

- For different sources with only the same first author (among all coauthors) and same date:
  - o **Include a shortened title** of work to distinguish between the sources:

General Format:	… (Lastname et al., "Shortened Title," Date) or … (Lastname et al., *Shortened Title*, Date)
Example:	… (Green et al., "Importance of Family," 2020) … (Green et al., *Popularity of Fast Food*, 2020)

Personal Communication

- To cite personal communication, follow the general format below:

General Format:	… (Name Lastname, pers. comm., Month Day, Year)
Example:	… (Victoria Reed, Instagram direct message to author, June 30, 2021)

Punctuation

In regards to punctuation, citations are always placed:
- **After** quotation marks (if any).
- **Before** other punctuation (if any).

For block quotes, citations are always placed **after** the closing punctuation mark with no extra period:

Example:	With his "Nothing will come of nothing; speak again" (1.1.92), Lear tries to draw from his youngest daughter an expression of filial devotion. There is evidence, for example, that the negative outcomes associated with family structure instability are more pronounced for young children as compared with older children (Sigle-Rushton and McLanahan 2004) and for boys as compared with girls (Cooper et al. 2011). The distinction between spirituality and religiosity is further clarified: Spirituality is more concerned with how an individual has a personal relationship to larger transcendent realities, such as the universe or God, whereas religiosity is more concerned with how an individual experiences a transcendent being and how this is expressed in a community or social organization. (Surname 2009, 34)

Placement

Citations Placed After Cited Material

When the **author's name does NOT appear** in the text (in signal phrase), citations are placed right after the cited material:

Example:	There is a huge influence of the environment in shaping people's behavior, personality, and perception about critical matters in marriage life (Simmons 2005).

When the **author's name** (even in possessive form) **appears** in the text (in signal phrase):
- **For summaries and paraphrases**, citations are always placed after the author's name:
  - Do not repeat author's name in the citation in this case.
  - Place the page number or any other locator in parentheses right after the cited material:

Example:	Griffin (2018) explains that many people who find themselves in domestic violence sometimes try to justify the abuser's actions (45).
	Griffin's (2008) study shows that many people who find themselves in domestic violence sometimes try to justify the abuser's actions (45).

Citations Placed either After Cited Material or After Author's Name

When the **author's name** (even in possessive form) **appears** in the text (in signal phrase):
- **For quotations**, citations may be placed either after the author's name or after the quotation:
  - Do not repeat author's name in the citation in this case.
  - Place the page number or any other locator in parentheses right after the cited material:

Example:	As Griffin (2018) points out, "They protect them, blame themselves, or even justify their actions thinking that things would get better" (49).
	As Griffin points out, "They protect them, blame themselves, or even justify their actions thinking that things would get better" (2018, 49).

Examples of citations when the author's name appears in the text:

	Author + Parenthetical Citation	Only Parenthetical Citation
1 Author	Scott (2021) indicated … (57)	… (Scott 2021, 57)
2 Authors	Torres and Williams (2018) point out … (34)	… (Torres and Williams 2018, 34)
3 Authors	Johnson, Adams, and Gray (2019) show … (102)	… (Johnson, Adams, and Gray 2019, 102)
4+ Authors	Green et al. (2020) argue … (19)	… (Green et al. 2020, 19)

Summary

		General Format	Example
1 Author		… (Lastname Date)	… (Scott 2021)
2 Authors		… (Lastname and Lastname Date)	… (Torres and Williams 2018)
3 Authors		… (Lastname, Lastname, and Lastname Date)	… (Johnson, Adams, and Gray 2019)
4+ Authors		… (Lastname et al. Date)	… (Green et al. 2020)
No Author		… (*Shortened Title* Date) or … ("Shortened Title" Date)	… (*Annoying Commercials* 2016) or … ("Importance of Family" 2020)
No Date		… (Lastname [Date?]) or … (Lastname, n.d.)	… (Murphy [1965?]) or … (Murphy, n.d.)
Page Number / Locator		… (Lastname Date, locator)	… (Miller 2015, 48) … (Miller 2015, 234–45) … (Miller 2015, 48, 234–45) … (Miller 2015, sec. 15)
Additional Information		… (Lastname Date, locator; additional information)	… (Adams 2004, 159; the interviewee wished to remain anonymous)
2+ Sources within the Same Citation		… (Lastname Date, locator; Lastname Date, locator; … ; Lastname Date, locator)	… (Johnson, Adams, and Gray 2019, 298; Miller 2015, 48)
Same Author and Date	All same authors	… (Lastname Datea) … (Lastname Dateb)	… (Watson 2010a) … (Watson 2010b)
	First same authors	… (Lastname et al., "Shortened Title," Date) or … (Lastname et al., *Shortened Title*, Date)	… (Green et al., "Importance of Family," 2020) … (Green et al., *Popularity of Fast Food*, 2020)
Personal Communication		… (Name Lastname, pers. comm., Month Day, Year)	… (Victoria Reed, Instagram direct message to author, June 30, 2021)

4.6 Bibliography / Reference List

~icago style requires to include **a list of sources** at the end of the paper in the form of:
- **Bibliography** (in Notes and Bibliography referencing system).
- **Reference list** (in Author-Date referencing system).

~e entries used in NB and AD systems are identical with the **only difference**:
- The year of publication is moved from the end of citation to the beginning (between the author and the title):

Notes and Bibliography **(NB)** Referencing System	Author-Date **(AD)** Referencing System
Bibliography	References
Perez, Amelia. *Effects of Pollution.* New York: Penguin Group, 2009.	Perez, Amelia. 2009. *Effects of Pollution.* New York: Penguin Group.

Formatting

- Bibliography/reference list appears at the very end of your paper on a separate page.
  - o Bibliography follows the endnotes (if any).
- Bibliography/reference list is **single-spaced**.
- Title the page "Bibliography" for NB referencing system or "References" for AD referencing system:
  - o Center the title at the top of page with no formatting (bold / italics / underscore).
- Leave **two blank lines** between "Bibliography" / "References" and the first entry.
- Bibliography/reference list includes all sources cited within the text:
  - o Do not include personal communications.
  - o Bibliography can additionally include sources that were consulted but not cited.
- Leave **one blank line** between entries.
- All major elements within entries are separated by periods.
- Entries are usually set smaller than the text.
- Entries are formatted with **hanging indents**:
  - o Flush the first line of entry with the left margin.
  - o Indent all subsequent lines of entry by 0.5 inches.
- Bibliography/reference list is **alphabetized** by the first letters of entries:
  - o Usually, entries are alphabetized by the author's last name.
  - o Entries with no author are alphabetized by titles.
    - ▪ Ignore the initial articles "The," "A," "An" when alphabetizing by titles.
  - o Entries that begin with the numbers (years) are alphabetized based on how the numbers (years) are spelled.
- Do not use abbreviations "p." or "pp." for page numbers within entries.

Elements of Entries

All entries in the bibliography/reference list normally include:
1. Author (or editor, translator, illustrator, creator, etc.).
2. Title (or description).
3. Other publication information.

- The entries with no author begin with the title (or descriptive phrase).
- **Skip any element** in the entry if the source does not provide full information.
- If any element is known for sure but is not provided within the source, include it in square brackets:
  - o If the element is not known for sure or is guessed, include it in square brackets with a questions mark:

Example:	[Miller, Isabella?]. *Current Affairs.* New York: Plume, 2018.

The order and spelling of authors' names should always match the cited source:
- The **first author's name** is ALWAYS **inverted** (Lastname, Firstname):
  - The last name appears first and is separated from the first name with a comma (for example: Baker, Oliver).
  - All following authors' and other contributors' names appear in normal order (Firstname Lastname).
- Always use **"and"** (not an ampersand "&") for several authors in an entry:
  - Always use a comma before "and."
- For the source with **1 to 10 authors**, include all names.
- For the source with **11+ authors**, include only the first seven names followed by "et al." (note that "et al." is preceded by an Oxford comma).
- For the source with an organization as author, use organization name instead of the author's name:
  - For the source published by institution, use the name of the department followed by the institution.
- For the source with no author, begin the entry with the following element (title):
  - Alternatively, use "Anonymous" or "Anon."
- To emphasize the editor (or any other contributor), treat the editor's name as the author's name:
  - Follow the editor's name with "ed." (or "eds." for plurals):

	General Format	**Example**
1 Author	Lastname, Firstname. ...	Smith, Olivia. ...
2-10 Authors	Lastname, Firstname, Firstname Lastname, [...] , Firstname Lastname, and Firstname Lastname. ...	Scott, Liam, and Zoey Torres. ... Williams, Noah, Hannah Adams, Luke Gray, and Eliana Jones. ...
11+ Authors	Lastname1, Firstname1, Firstname2 Lastname2, Firstname3 Lastname3, Firstname4 Lastname4, Firstname5 Lastname5, Firstname6 Lastname6, and Firstname7 Lastname7, et al. ...	Baker, Oliver, Hazel Ramirez, Grayson Brown, Anna Gonzalez, Landon James, Sophia Davis, William Nelson, et al. ...
Organization as Author	Organization. ...	World Medical Relief. ...
No Author	Omit the author or use "Anonymous"	Omit the author or use "Anonymous"
Editor / Translator as Author	Lastname, Firstname, ed. ... Lastname, Firstname, Firstname Lastname, [...] , Firstname Lastname, and Firstname Lastname, eds. ...	Perez, Amelia, ed. ... Sanders, Benjamin, Theodore Mitchell, and Ruby Kelly, eds. ...

2. Title

Include full titles and subtitles in bibliography/reference list:
- Titles and subtitles get **headline-style** capitalization.
- Titles of larger works (full volumes) are **italicized**:
  - *Books,*
  - *Periodicals,*
  - *Movies,*
  - *TV Shows*, etc.
- Titles of shorter works (items within full volumes) are enclosed in **double quotation marks**:
  - "Chapters,"
  - "Articles,"
  - "Scenes,"
  - "Episodes," etc.

For more information on formatting titles, check chapter "4.3 Titles of Works" in this guide.

3. Publication Information

Publishers Cities

- For **widely known** city (New York, London, etc.), list **only the name** of the city.
- For little-known city, list the name of the city followed by the US state/province abbreviation or country name according to standard postal abbreviations.
- If there are 2+ publishers cities, include only the first city listed:

Example:	New York
	Menlo Park, CA
	London
	Newton Abbot, United Kingdom

Publishers Names

- The publisher name should have a **brief** form:
  - Omit the words "The," "Publishers," "Inc.," and "Co." from the publisher name.
  - Retain the words "Press" and "Books."
  - Do not abbreviate the publisher name:

Original Publisher Name:	Sterling Publishing Co., Inc.
Preferred Publisher Name in Chicago Style:	Sterling

Dates of Publication

- For the sources that require including month of publication, write the month in full (**do not abbreviate** it).
- For the sources with no date of publication, use the abbreviation "n.d."
- For the sources with no certain date of publication, use the abbreviation "ca." (for circa):

Example:	2021
	October 2021
	October 23, 2020
	n.d.
	ca. 1755

- For **online** sources, the date of publication can be substituted with the date of revision / update / modification:
  - Use respective phrase to distinguish: Published / Updated / Last modified:

Example:	WD Corporation. "Free Grammar Software." Grammar Plus. Updated May 13, 2021. https://www.grammarplus.com/soft/free/09346.

Access Dates

- For online sources with **NO** available date of publication / revision / modification, **include access dates**:
  - Include access date before DOI / Database / URL:

Example:	East Delta University. "Liberty and Anarchy." Accessed September 2, 2021. http://www.eastdelta.edu/.

- For online sources with available date of publication / revision / modification, access dates are usually NOT required but they **may be included if instructed** by your institution.

For online sources, include DOI / database / URL at the end of entry to help readers locate the sources:
- **DOI is preferred** over databases and URLs:
  - DOI is a digital object identifier.
  - Most academic sources / journal articles have DOIs.
- If no DOI is available, use the **database** name instead:
- If the source is not from a database, use **URL** instead:
  - URL is Uniform Resource Locator.
  - All online sources have URLs.
- Begin both DOIs and URLs with the protocol **"http://"** or **"https://"**:

Example:	https://doi.org/1069.109957.6758.4779
	https://www.amazon.com/Appearance-Publishers/e/B091TLWPW9/

URLs and DOIs Line Breaks

Chicago style has specific requirements on URLs and DOIs line breaks in printed works:
- DOIs and URLs lines can be broken:
  - **Before** single slash (/), period (.), comma (,), hyphen (-), underline (_), question mark (?), number sign (#), percent symbol (%), or tilde (~).
  - **After** double slash (//) or colon (:).
  - Before or after ampersand (&) or equals sign (=).

2+ Works by the Same Author

For several works by the one author, use **3 em dashes** (————) to replace the same author's name as in previous entry:
- Entries are alphabetized by the titles of works:
  - Ignore initial articles "The," "A," "An":

Example:	Watson, Jonathan. *The Angry Road.* London: Hyphen Press, 2010.
	————. *Policeman.* London: Routledge, 2010.
	————. *Religion.* London: Cape, 2016.

Chicago style (17th edition) **discourages** the use of 3 em dashes (————):
- Instead, format entries as usual providing the author's name each time.
- Entries are alphabetized by the titles of works:
  - Ignore initial articles "The," "A," "An":

Example:	Watson, Jonathan. *The Angry Road.* London: Hyphen Press, 2010.
	Watson, Jonathan. *Policeman.* London: Routledge, 2010.
	Watson, Jonathan. *Religion.* London: Cape, 2016.

- In AD referencing system, if 2+ works by the same author have the same date of publication, **assign letters** (a, b, c, ...) to the dates:

Example:	Watson, Jonathan. 2010a. *The Angry Road.* London: Hyphen Press.
	Watson, Jonathan. 2010b. *Policeman.* London: Routledge.
	Watson, Jonathan. 2016. *Religion.* London: Cape.

5.0 NB SYSTEM: NOTES / BIBLIOGRAPHY EXAMPLES

This chapter contains general format and examples for citing sources:
- Remember that notes and bibliography entries are formatted differently:
  o In notes: major elements are separated by commas.
  o In bibliography: major elements are separated by a period and the first author's name is inverted.

PAY ATTENTION TO:

1. Capitalization
2. Punctuation
3. Italics
4. Quotation marks

SKIP ANY ELEMENT IF IT IS NOT APPLICABLE TO YOUR SPECIFIC SOURCE

5.1 Authors

- In bibliography, the first author's name is ALWAYS **inverted** (Lastname, Firstname):
  o Only the first author's name is inverted.
- In notes (footnotes/endnotes), the author's name is NEVER inverted.

TIP TO REMEMBER FORMATTING AUTHORS' NAMES:
- Remember the "Z-structure" when listing the first author name in notes, shortened notes, and bibliography entries:

Note	#. Firstname Lastname, ...
Shortened Note	#. Lastname, ...
Bibliography	Lastname, Firstname. ...

- All following authors' and other contributors' names appear in normal order (Firstname Lastname).

1 Author

	General Format	**Example**
Note: -Endnote -Footnote	#. Firstname Lastname, *Title: Subtitle* (City: Publisher, Year), page.	1. Olivia Smith, *Water Scarcity* (New York: Aspen, 2019), 34.
Shortened Note	#. Lastname, *Shortened Title,* page.	2. Smith, *Water Scarcity*, 45
Bibliography	Lastname, Firstname. *Title: Subtitle*. City: Publisher, Year.	Smith, Olivia. *Water Scarcity*. New York: Aspen, 2019.

2 Authors

	General Format	**Example**
Note: -Endnote -Footnote	#. Firstname Lastname and Firstname Lastname, *Title: Subtitle* (City: Publisher, Year), page.	1. Liam Scott and Zoey Torres, *Uneasy Lies the Head That Wears the Crown* (Boston: Houghton, 2008), 78.
Shortened Note	#. Lastname and Lastname, *Shortened Title,* page.	2. Scott and Torres, *Uneasy Lies the Head,* 79.
Bibliography	Lastname, Firstname, and Firstname Lastname. *Title: Subtitle*. City: Publisher, Year.	Scott, Liam, and Zoey Torres. *Uneasy Lies the Head That Wears the Crown*. Boston: Houghton, 2008.

3 Authors

- In both notes and bibliography, include the **names of all authors**:
  - Use a comma before "and" for the final author:

	General Format	Example
Note: -Endnote -Footnote	#. Firstname Lastname, Firstname Lastname, and Firstname Lastname, *Title: Subtitle* (City: Publisher, Year), page.	1. Julian Johnson, Caroline Green, and Aaron Peterson, *A Stitch in Time Saves Nine* (Reading, MA: Addison-Wesley, 2012), 99.
Shortened Note	#. Lastname, Lastname, and Lastname, *Shortened Title*, page.	2. Johnson, Green, and Peterson, *Stitch in Time*, 103.
Bibliography	Lastname, Firstname, Firstname Lastname, and Firstname Lastname. *Title: Subtitle*. City: Publisher, Year.	Johnson, Julian, Caroline Green, and Aaron Peterson. *A Stitch in Time Saves Nine*. Reading, MA: Addison-Wesley, 2012.

4–10 Authors

- In notes, list the first author's name followed by "et al."
- In bibliography, include the **names of all authors**:
  - Alternatively, **if the space is limited**, Chicago allows following AMA style guidelines (include only the first three authors followed by "et al." if there are more than six authors):

	General Format	Example
Note: -Endnote -Footnote	#. Firstname Lastname et al., *Title: Subtitle* (City: Publisher, Year), page.	1. Noah Williams et al., *Election and Democracy* (New York: Harper Perennial, 1997), 43.
Shortened Note	#. Lastname et al., *Shortened Title*, page.	2. Williams et al., *Election and Democracy*, 49.
Bibliography	Lastname, Firstname, Firstname Lastname, [...], Firstname Lastname, and Firstname Lastname. *Title: Subtitle*. City: Publisher, Year.	Williams, Noah, Hannah Adams, Luke Gray, and Eliana Jones. *Election and Democracy*. New York: Harper Perennial, 1997.

11+ Authors

- In notes, list the first author's name followed by "et al."
- In bibliography, include the **first seven authors** followed by "et al.":
  - Alternatively, **if the space is limited**, Chicago allows following AMA style guidelines (include the first three authors followed by "et al."):

	General Format	Example
Note: -Endnote -Footnote	#. Firstname Lastname et al., *Title: Subtitle* (City: Publisher, Year), page.	1. Oliver Baker et al., *Demonetization* (Albany, NY: Delmar Thomson Learning, 2004), 8.
Shortened Note	#. Lastname et al., *Shortened Title*, page.	2. Baker et al., *Demonetization*, 76.
Bibliography	Lastname1, Firstname1, Firstname2 Lastname2, Firstname3 Lastname3, Firstname4 Lastname4, Firstname5 Lastname5, Firstname6 Lastname6, and Firstname7 Lastname7, et al. *Title: Subtitle*. City: Publisher, Year.	Baker, Oliver, Hazel Ramirez, Grayson Brown, Anna Gonzalez, Landon James, Sophia Davis, William Nelson, et al. *Demonetization*. Albany, NY: Delmar Thomson Learning, 2006.

Organization as Author

- Use the group's name in place of the author's name if the author is an organization, agency, association, corporation, government, etc.:

	General Format	Example
Note: -Endnote -Footnote	#. Organization, *Title: Subtitle* (City: Publisher, Year), page.	1. World Medical Relief, *Television in our Daily Life* (Tustin, CA: WC Publishing, 2020), 476.
Shortened Note	#. Organization, *Shortened Title*, page.	2. World Medical Relief, *Television*, 60.
Bibliography	Organization. *Title: Subtitle*. City: Publisher, Year.	World Medical Relief. *Television in our Daily Life*. Tustin, CA: WC Publishing, 2020.

No Author

- For the source with no author, omit the author's name and begin the entry with the source's next element (title):
  - When alphabetizing entries in the bibliography, **ignore initial articles** "The," "A," "An".
- EXCEPT: For newspapers articles with no author:
  - In bibliography, **move the newspaper title** into place of the author:

	General Format	Example
Note: -Endnote -Footnote	#. *Title: Subtitle* (City: Publisher, Year), page.	1. *How to Eradicate Corruption* (Munich: K. G. Saur, 2005), 56.
Shortened Note	#. *Shortened Title*, page.	2. *How to Eradicate Corruption*, 58.
Bibliography	*Title: Subtitle*. City: Publisher, Year.	*How to Eradicate Corruption*. Munich: K. G. Saur, 2005.

- Alternatively, use "Anonymous" or "Anon." in place of the author's name:
  - Chicago style recommends avoiding the use of "Anonymous" or "Anon." unless the source itself is authored by Anonymous:

	General Format	Example
Note: -Endnote -Footnote	#. Anonymous. *Title: Subtitle* (City: Publisher, Year), page.	1. Anonymous. *How to Eradicate Corruption* (Munich: K. G. Saur, 2005), 56.
Shortened Note	#. Anonymous. *Shortened Title*, page.	2. Anonymous. *How to Eradicate Corruption*, 58.
Bibliography	Anonymous. *Title: Subtitle*. City: Publisher, Year.	Anonymous. *How to Eradicate Corruption*. Munich: K. G. Saur, 2005.

Pseudonyms

Widely known pseudonyms are treated as the authors' real names.
- If the author's real name is of interest to readers, include the **real name in square brackets** after the pseudonym.

Descriptive pseudonyms are followed by "pseud." in square brackets:
- Omit initial "The," "A," or "An" in pseudonyms.
- In notes, "pseud." is usually omitted:

	General Format	Example
Note: -Endnote -Footnote	#. Pseudonym, *Title: Subtitle* (City: Publisher, Year), page.	1. Dizzaz. *The Road Rage* (London: Hyphen Press, 1995), 29.
Shortened Note	#. Pseudonym, *Shortened Title*, page.	2. Dizzaz. *Road Rage*, 302.
Bibliography	Pseudonym [pseud.]. *Title: Subtitle*. City: Publisher, Year.	Dizzaz [pseud.]. *The Road Rage*. London: Hyphen Press, 1995.
	Pseudonym [real name]. *Title: Subtitle*. City: Publisher, Year.	Dizzaz [Watson, Jonathan]. *The Road Rage*. London: Hyphen Press, 1995.

- If the author's name is known but is not listed in the source itself, use **square brackets** around the author's name:
  - Use a **question mark** if the author's name is guessed to highlight uncertainty:

	General Format	Example
Note: -Endnote -Footnote	#. [Firstname Lastname], *Title: Subtitle* (City: Publisher, Year), page.	1. [Isabella Miller?], *Current Affairs* (New York: Plume, 2018), 87.
Shortened Note	#. [Lastname], *Shortened Title*, page.	2. [Miller?], *Current Affairs*, 193.
Bibliography	[Lastname, Firstname]. *Title: Subtitle*. City: Publisher, Year.	[Miller, Isabella?]. *Current Affairs*. New York: Plume, 2018.

5.2 Books

General Guidelines

- Use headline-style capitalization for titles and subtitles.
- Use the most recent edition of the book:
    - For an edition other than the first, include the edition number after the title.
- Include **other contributors**, such as editors, translators, illustrators, etc.
- The publisher name should have **a brief form**:
    - Omit the words "The," "Publishers," "Inc.," and "Co." from the publisher name.
    - Retain the words "Press" and "Books."
    - Do not abbreviate the publishers names.
- If there are 2+ publishers cities, **include only the first city** listed:
    - For widely known city (New York, London, etc.), list only the name of the city.
    - For little-known city, list the name of the city followed by the US state/province abbreviation or country name according to standard postal abbreviations.
- If the book is available online, include DOI/Database/URL.

	General Format	Example
Note: -Endnote -Footnote	#. Firstname Lastname, *Title: Subtitle*, # ed., trans./ed. Firstname Lastname (City: Publisher, Year), page, DOI/Database/URL.	1. Charlotte Carter, *Encountering Distant Voices: Exploring the Role of Warrior as an Aspect of Peace Studies*, 4th ed., trans. Oliver Stewart (New York: Aspen, 2009), 59, NetLibrary.
Shortened Note	#. Lastname, *Shortened Title*, page.	2. Carter, *Distant Voices,* 98.
Bibliography	Lastname, Firstname. *Title: Subtitle*, # ed. Translated/Edited by Firstname Lastname. City: Publisher, Year. DOI/Database/URL.	Carter, Charlotte. *Encountering Distant Voices: Exploring the Role of Warrior as an Aspect of Peace Studies*. 4th ed. Translated by Oliver Stewart. New York: Aspen, 2009. NetLibrary.

Book

	General Format	Example
Note: -Endnote -Footnote	#. Firstname Lastname, *Title: Subtitle* (City: Publisher, Year), page.	1 James Brooks, *Favorite Athlete* (New York: Pocket Books, 2018), 43.
Shortened Note	#. Lastname, *Shortened Title*, page.	2. Brooks, *Favorite Athlete*, 64.
Bibliography	Lastname, Firstname. *Title: Subtitle*. City: Publisher, Year.	Brooks, James J. *Favorite Athlete*. New York: Pocket Books, 2018.

Book (Edition Other Than the First)

- Include the edition number after the title (ordinal number + "ed."):
    - In notes, use a comma to separate the edition number from the title.
    - In bibliography, use a period to separate the edition number from the title:

	General Format	Example
Note: -Endnote -Footnote	#. Firstname Lastname, *Title: Subtitle*, # ed. (City: Publisher, Year), page.	1. Violet Wilson, *Songs and Dances of Divinity*, 3rd ed. (Boston: Houghton, 2012), 47.
Shortened Note	#. Lastname, *Shortened Title*, page.	2. Wilson, *Divinity*, 46.
Bibliography	Lastname, Firstname. *Title: Subtitle*. # ed. City: Publisher, Year.	Wilson, Violet. *Songs and Dances of Divinity*. 3rd ed. Boston: Houghton, 2012.

Book (Edited / Translated / Illustrated)

- In notes, **abbreviate** contributors' titles ("ed." for editor, "eds." for editors, "trans." for translator, "illus." for illustrator, etc.).
- In bibliography, **spell out** contributors' titles ("Edited by", "Translated by," "Illustrated by," etc.).

Option 1 (Preferred)

- Generally, begin the entry with the author's name and title, followed by the contributors' names:

	General Format	Example
Note: -Endnote -Footnote	#. Author's Firstname Lastname, *Title: Subtitle*, ed./trans./illus. Firstname Lastname (City: Publisher, Year), page.	1. Theodore Mitchell, *Effects of Pollution,* ed. Amelia Perez (New York: Penguin Group, 2009) 34. 2. Ruby Kelly, *The Nicest Place We Would Need to Go*, trans. Benjamin Sanders (San Francisco Chronicle Books, 2004), 66. 3. Hunter Moore, *Traveling as a Hobby,* illus. Lillian Taylor (Tustin, CA: WC Publishing, 2020), 223.
Shortened Note	#. Author's Lastname, *Shortened Title*, page.	4. Mitchell, *Pollution*, 46. 5. Kelly, *Nicest Place*, 78. 6. Moore, *Traveling as a Hobby*, 228.
Bibliography	Author's Lastname, Firstname. *Title: Subtitle*. Edited/Translated/Illustrated by Firstname Lastname. City: Publisher, Year.	Mitchell, Theodore. *Effects of Pollution.* Edited by Amelia Perez. New York: Penguin Group, 2009. Kelly, Ruby. *The Nicest Place We Would Need to Go.* Translated by Benjamin Sanders. San Francisco: Chronicle Books, 2004. Moore, Hunter. *Traveling as a Hobby.* Illustrated by Lillian Taylor. Tustin, CA: WC Publishing, 2020.

Option 2 (Emphasize Contributors)

- For the sources where contributors are of the main interest to readers (for example, if the paper focuses on different translations), use the contributors' names instead of the author's name:
  - Follow contributors' names with their titles, such as "ed." or "eds." or "trans.":

	General Format	Example
Note: -Endnote -Footnote	#. Editor/Translator/Illustrator's Firstname Lastname, ed./trans./illus., *Title: Subtitle* (City: Publisher, Year), page.	1. Amelia Perez, ed., *Effects of Pollution* (New York: Penguin Group, 2009), 34. 2. Benjamin Sanders, trans., *The Nicest Place We Would Need to Go* (San Francisco: Chronicle Books, 2004), 66.
Shortened Note	#. Editor/Translator/Illustrator's Lastname, *Shortened Title*, page.	4. Perez, *Pollution*, 46. 5. Sanders, *Nicest Place*, 78.
Bibliography	Editor/Translator/Illustrator's Lastname, Firstname, ed./trans./illus. *Title: Subtitle*. City: Publisher, Year.	Perez, Amelia, ed. *Effects of Pollution.* New York: Penguin Group, 2009. Sanders, Benjamin, trans. *The Nicest Place We Would Need to Go.* San Francisco: Chronicle Books, 2004.

Introduction / Preface / Afterword in a Book

- Note that bibliography entry includes the **full page range** of introduction / preface / afterword, etc.:

	General Format	Example
Note: -Endnote -Footnote	#. Firstname Lastname, introduction to *Title: Subtitle* (City: Publisher, Year), page.	1. Gabriel Roberts, introduction to *Lata Mangeshkar* (London: Routledge, 1999), xii.
Shortened Note	#. Lastname, *Shortened Title*, page.	2. Roberts, *Title*, xiii.
Bibliography	Lastname, Firstname. Introduction to *Title: Subtitle*, page range. City: Publisher, Year.	Roberts, Gabriel. Introduction to *Lata Mangeshkar*, xi–xv. London: Routledge, 1999.

Chapter in a Book

- Note that the bibliography entry includes the **full page range** of chapter.

Option 1 (Preferred)

	General Format	Example
Note: -Endnote -Footnote	#. Firstname Lastname, "Chapter Title," in *Title: Subtitle* (City: Publisher, Year), page.	1. Kennedy Price, "Exploring the Role of Warrior as an Aspect of Peace Studies," in *Encountering Distant Voices* (Melbourne: Cambridge University Press, 2017), 314.
Shortened Note	#. Lastname, "Shortened Chapter Title," page.	2. Price, "Role of Warrior," 317.
Bibliography	Lastname, Firstname. "Chapter Title." In *Title: Subtitle,* page range. City: Publisher, Year.	Price, Kennedy. "Exploring the Role of Warrior as an Aspect of Peace Studies." In *Encountering Distant Voices*, 310–33. Melbourne: Cambridge University Press, 2017.

Option 2 (Emphasize the Entire Book)

	General Format	Example
Note: -Endnote -Footnote	#. Firstname Lastname, *Title: Subtitle* (City: Publisher, Year), page.	1. Kennedy Price, *Encountering Distant Voices* (Melbourne: Cambridge University Press, 2017), 314.
Shortened Note	#. Lastname, *Shortened Title,* page.	2. Price, *Encountering Distant Voices*, 317.
Bibliography	Lastname, Firstname. *Title: Subtitle*. City: Publisher, Year. See esp. chap. #, "Chapter Title."	Price, Kennedy. *Encountering Distant Voices*. Melbourne: Cambridge University Press, 2017. See esp. chap. 8, "Exploring the Role of Warrior as an Aspect of Peace Studies."

Chapter in a Book with Various Authored Chapters / Essay in a Book / Work in Anthology

There are edited books with chapters that are written by different authors. There are 2 methods to cite such sources:
1. Cite specific chapter / essay with its author.
2. Cite the entire book / collection.

Works with translators are treated similarly.

Option 1 (Specific Chapter / Essay)

- When citing specific chapter, begin the entry with the chapter's author followed by the chapter title:
  - Include the title of the entire book / collection followed by the book's editor:

	General Format	Example
Note: -Endnote -Footnote	#. Chapter Author's Firstname Lastname, "Chapter Title," in *Title: Subtitle*, ed. Editor's Firstname Lastname (City: Publisher, Year), page.	1. Leo Collins, "The Dance of Healing," in *Religion and Psychology*, ed. Cameron Turner (Boston: D. R. Godine, 2006), 319.
Shortened Note	#. Chapter Author's Lastname, "Shortened Chapter Title," page.	2. Collins, "Dance of Healing," 328.
Bibliography	Chapter Author's Lastname, Firstname. "Chapter Title." In *Title: Subtitle*, edited by Editor's Firstname Lastname, page range. City: Publisher, Year.	Collins, Leo. "The Dance of Healing." In *Religion and Psychology*, edited by Cameron Turner, 289–347. Boston: D. R. Godine, 2006.

Option 2 (Entire Book / Collection)

- When citing the entire book / collection, include only book's editor (in place of the author) and the title of the book:

	General Format	Example
Note: -Endnote -Footnote	#. Editor's Firstname Lastname, ed., *Title: Subtitle* (City: Publisher, Year), page.	1. Cameron Turner, ed., *Religion and Psychology* (Boston: D. R. Godine, 2006), 319.
Shortened Note	#. Editor's Lastname, *Shortened Title*, page.	2. Turner, *Religion and Psychology*, 328.
Bibliography	Editor's Lastname, Firstname, ed. *Title: Subtitle*. City: Publisher, Year.	Turner, Cameron, ed. *Religion and Psychology*. Boston: D. R. Godine, 2006.

Multi-Volume Book

	General Format	Example
Note: -Endnote -Footnote	#. Firstname Lastname, *Title: Subtitle* (City: Publisher, Year), volume:page.	1. Mia Bennett, *Systematic Theology* (Los Angeles: Acrobat Books, 2004), 4:122.
Shortened Note	#. Lastname, *Shortened Title*, volume:page.	2. Bennett, *Theology*, 4:170.
Bibliography	Lastname, Firstname. *Title: Subtitle*. Vol. #. City: Publisher, Year.	Bennett, Mia. *Systematic Theology*. Vol. 4. Los Angeles: Acrobat Books, 2004.

E-Book

- Electronic books (e-books) are treated as any other books with the addition of **media** (Kindle, EPUB, etc.):
  - o As long as e-books might not have fixed pages and the pagination may differ on devices, use **any other locator** (section title, chapter number, paragraph number, etc.):

	General Format	Example
Note: -Endnote -Footnote	#. Firstname Lastname, *Title: Subtitle* (City: Publisher, Year), page, Media.	1. Lucas Thomas, *Learning to Play Piano* (New York: Columbia University Press, 2018), loc. 238 of 4928, Kindle.
Shortened Note	#. Lastname, *Shortened Title*, page.	2. Thomas, *Learning to Play Piano*, loc. 238 of 4928.
Bibliography	Lastname, Firstname. *Title: Subtitle*. City: Publisher, Year. Media.	Thomas, Lucas. *Learning to Play Piano*. New York: Columbia University Press, 2018. Kindle.

Online Book

- For online books, include library **database or distributor** (EBSCO, Ebrary, etc.), DOI, or URL:
  - o As long as online books might not have pages or the pagination may differ on devices, use **any other locator** (section title, chapter number, paragraph number, etc.):

	General Format	Example
Note: -Endnote -Footnote	#. Firstname Lastname, *Title: Subtitle*, (City: Publisher, Year), page, DOI/Database/URL.	1. Zoe Phillips, *Monuments* (New York: Harper Perennial, 2005), 274, Ebrary. 2. Anthony Wood, *An Ideal Student* (Cambridge, MA: MIT Press, 2012), under "Examination Fever," Google Books, https://books.google.com/books?isbn=98738492755. 3. Ivy Jackson, *Obesity in America* (New York: Dover, 2018), chap. 6, https://doi.org/1043.5596.0477.
Shortened Note	#. Lastname, *Shortened Title*, page.	4. Phillips, *Monuments*, 274. 5. Wood, *Ideal Student*, under "Examination Fever." 6. Jackson, *Obesity in America*, chap. 6.
Bibliography	Lastname, Firstname. *Title: Subtitle*. City: Publisher, Year. DOI/Database/URL.	Phillips, Zoe. *Monuments*. New York: Harper Perennial, 2005. Ebrary. Wood, Anthony. *An Ideal Student*. Cambridge, MA: MIT Press, 2012. Google Books. https://books.google.com/books?isbn=98738492755. Jackson, Ivy. *Obesity in America*. New York: Dover, 2018. https://doi.org/1043.5596.0477.

Audiobook / Poetry Reading

- If the author is also the reader, replace "read by Reader's Firstname Lastname" with "read by the author":

	General Format	Example
Note: -Endnote -Footnote	#. Firstname Lastname, *Title: Subtitle*, read by Reader's Firstname Lastname (City: Publisher, Year), Medium, running time.	1. Connor Campbell, *Farewell in High School*, read by Eva Miller (London: Hyphen Audiobooks, 2007), Audible audio ed., 17 hr., 43 min.
Shortened Note	#. Lastname, *Shortened Title*.	2. Campbell, *Farewell in High School*.
Bibliography	Lastname, Firstname. *Title: Subtitle*. Read by Reader's Firstname Lastname. City: Publisher, Year. Medium, running time.	Campbell, Connor. *Farewell in High School*. Read by Eva Miller. London: Hyphen Audiobooks, 2007. Audible audio ed., 17 hr., 43 min.

Pamphlet

- Pamphlets are treated as books:
  - o Provide as much information as possible to identify the pamphlet:

	General Format	Example
Note: -Endnote -Footnote	*#. Title: Subtitle* (City: Publisher, Year), page.	1. *Deep Breathing: A Means for Autistic People to Reconnect with Their Bodies* (Washington, DC: Island Press, 2001), 2.
Shortened Note	*#. Shortened Title*, page.	2. *Deep Breathing*, 6.
Bibliography	*Title: Subtitle*. City: Publisher, Year.	*Deep Breathing: A Means for Autistic People to Reconnect with Their Bodies*. Washington, DC: Island Press, 2001.

Scriptural Sources / Sacred Texts (Bible, Koran, etc.)

Scriptural sources are cited only in notes (and are not included in bibliography):
- Include the book title.
- Do not include page numbers:
  - o Instead include **chapter and verse with a colon between** (chapter:verse) or use another similar system.

When citing the Bible, specify the version as supplementary information in parentheses:
- Abbreviate subsequent mentions of the version of the Bible:

	General Format	Example
Note	#. Book chapter:verse (Version).	1. 1 Samuel 1:21–23 (New Jerusalem Bible).
Shortened Note	#. Book chapter:verse (Version Abbreviation).	2. Genesis 1:1–11 (NJB).

Classical Texts / Classic Plays / Epic Poems

Classical primary sources are usually cited only in notes (and are not included in bibliography):
- Instead of using page numbers, follow the **author's established scheme** such as:
  - o For an epic poem – "book.line" format.
  - o For classic plays – "act.scene.line." format.
  - o For other classical texts – "book.chapter.section" format, etc.
  - o Use **Arabic** numerals (1, 2, 3, …):

	General Format	Example
Note: -Endnote -Footnote	*#. Author, Title*, number.number.number. *#. Author, Title*, trans./ed. Firstname Lastname (City: Publisher, Year), number.number.number.	1. Shakespeare, *All's Well That Ends Well*, 2.3.199–204. 2. Plato, *Euthyphro*, trans. John Healey (New York: Thames and Hudson, 1998), 14.7.
Shortened Note	*#. Author, Shortened Title*, number.number.number.	3. Shakespeare, *All's Well*, 2.3.220. 4. Plato, *Euthyphro*, 14.7.
Bibliography	Author. *Title*. Translated/Edited by Firstname Lastname. City: Publisher, Year.	Shakespeare, William. *All's Well That Ends Well*. Edited by Mason Barnes. Boston: Houghton, 2017. Plato. *Euthyphro*. Translated by Logan Bailey. New York: Thames and Hudson, 1998.

- If the numbering system might be unclear to readers, use labels ("bk.," "act," "sc.," "line," etc.) for the first note:

	General Format	Example
Note	*#. Author, Title*, act #, sc. #, line #.	1. Shakespeare, *All's Well That Ends Well*, act 2, sc. 3, line 199.

5.3 Articles in Periodicals

General Guidelines

Periodicals include magazines, newspapers, and journals:
- Magazines and newspapers issues are usually identified by day, month, and year.
- Journals issues are usually identified by volume and issue and month/season and year.

When citing an article from periodical:
- **Article** titles are enclosed **in double quotation marks**.
- **Periodical** titles are **italicized**.

Magazine Articles

Titles:
- Article titles are enclosed in double quotation marks.
- Magazine titles are italicized.

Date of publication:
- For weekly or bi-weekly magazines, include the full date (Month Day, Year).
- For monthly or bi-monthly magazines, include only month and year (Month Year).

Page numbers:
- In notes, include the **exact page number** of the cited material.
- In bibliography, include the **full page range** of the article.
- For online articles with no available pages, simply omit pages (do not include any other locator):

	General Format	Example
Note: -Endnote -Footnote	#. Firstname Lastname, "Title of Article," Column Title if any, *Title of Magazine*, Month Day, Year, page, URL/Database.	1. Harper Barnes, "Behavioral and Brain Science," Science, *Health*, April 14, 2021, http://healthmagazine.com/scn/99283646/.
Shortened Note	#. Lastname, "Shortened Title of Article," page.	2. Barnes, "Behavioral and Brain Science."
Bibliography	Lastname, Firstname. "Title of Article." Column Title if any. *Title of Magazine*, Month Day, Year, page range. URL/Database.	Barnes, Harper. "Behavioral and Brain Science." Science. *Health*, April 14, 2021. http://healthmagazine.com/scn/99283646/.

Print Article

	General Format	Example
Note: -Endnote -Footnote	#. Firstname Lastname, "Title of Article," *Title of Magazine*, Month Day, Year, page.	1. Mason White, "Nonviolence in Action," *Peace Studies*, March 2020, 49.
Shortened Note	#. Lastname, "Shortened Title of Article," page.	2. White, "Nonviolence in Action," 49.
Bibliography	Lastname, Firstname. "Title of Article." *Title of Magazine*, Month Day, Year, page range.	White, Mason. "Nonviolence in Action." *Peace Studies*, March 2020, 39–53.

Online Article from the Internet

- For online magazine articles, include a URL or database:

	General Format	**Example**
Note: -Endnote -Footnote	#. Firstname Lastname, "Title of Article," *Title of Magazine*, Month Day, Year, page, URL/Database.	1. Stella Parker, "Mango Fruit," *Food and Nutrition*, April 19, 2020, http://www.foodnnutrition.com/articles/30568270.
Shortened Note	#. Lastname, "Shortened Title of Article," page.	2. Parker, "Mango Fruit."
Bibliography	Lastname, Firstname. "Title of Article." *Title of Magazine*, Month Day, Year, page range. URL/Database.	Parker, Stella. "Mango Fruit." *Food and Nutrition*, April 19, 2020. http://www.foodnnutrition.com/articles/3056 8270.

Online Article via Mobile App

	General Format	**Example**
Note: -Endnote -Footnote	#. Firstname Lastname, "Title of Article," *Title of Magazine* (mobile app), Month Day, Year.	1. Dylan Ross, "Inter School Competition," *Being in the World* (iPhone app), June 2008.
Shortened Note	#. Lastname, "Shortened Title of Article."	2. Ross, "Inter School Competition."
Bibliography	Lastname, Firstname. "Title of Article." *Title of Magazine* (mobile app), Month Day, Year.	Ross, Dylan. "Inter School Competition." *Being in the World* (iPhone app), June 2008.

Online Article from a Library Database

	General Format	**Example**
Note: -Endnote -Footnote	#. Firstname Lastname, "Title of Article," *Title of Magazine*, Month Day, Year, page, Database.	1. Ariana Harris, "Genetic Engineering," *FG Studying*, May 12, 2020, 35, FG Studying.
Shortened Note	#. Lastname, "Shortened Title of Article," page.	2. Harris, "Genetic Engineering," 39.
Bibliography	Lastname, Firstname. "Title of Article." *Title of Magazine*, Month Day, Year, page range. Database.	Harris, Ariana. "Genetic Engineering," *FG Studying*, May 12, 2020, 26–47. FG Studying.

Newspaper Articles

Newspaper articles are usually cited only in notes:
- Include bibliography entries only if instructed.

Titles:
- Article titles are enclosed in double quotation marks.
- Newspaper titles are italicized:
  - **Omit the initial article "The"** from newspaper titles.

Date of publication:
- Always include the full date (Month Day, Year).

Page numbers:
- Generally, **page numbers can be omitted**. However, if you decide to include page numbers:
  - In notes, include the exact page number of the cited material.
  - In bibliography, include the full page range of the article.
- For online articles with no available pages, simply omit pages (do not include any other locator).

Specific requirements:
- Include **newspaper edition** if available (for example, California edition).
- Include **newspaper section** for print articles (for example, sec. A).
- Omit the initial article "The" from newspaper titles.
- For articles with no author, in bibliography use the newspaper title in place of the author.
- For **little-known American newspapers**, **include city** after the newspaper title in parentheses:

	General Format	Example
Note: -Endnote -Footnote	#. Firstname Lastname, "Title of Article," Column Title if any, *Title of Newspaper* (City), Month Day, Year, edition, section, page, URL/Database.	1. Santiago Evans, "A Railway Accident," This Week, *Transportation Technologies* (Haven, CT), May 14, 2018, Haven edition, sec. D.
Shortened Note	#. Lastname, "Shortened Title of Article," page.	2. Evans, "A Railway Accident."
Bibliography	Lastname, Firstname. "Title of Article." Column Title if any. *Title of Newspaper* (City), Month Day, Year, edition, section, page range. URL/Database.	Evans, Santiago. "A Railway Accident." This Week. *Transportation Technologies* (Haven, CT), May 14, 2018, Haven edition, sec. D.

Print Article

	General Format	Example
Note: -Endnote -Footnote	#. Firstname Lastname, "Title of Article," *Title of Newspaper*, Month Day, Year, page.	1. Evelyn Henderson, "Effects of Social Networking Sites," *Washington Post*, January 16, 2020, 12.
Shortened Note	#. Lastname, "Shortened Title of Article," page.	2. Henderson, "Social Networking Sites," 12.
Bibliography	Lastname, Firstname. "Title of Article." *Title of Newspaper*, Month Day, Year, page range.	Henderson, Evelyn. "Effects of Social Networking Sites." *Washington Post*, January 16, 2020, 12–13.

- For online newspaper articles, include a URL:

	General Format	Example
Note: -Endnote -Footnote	#. Firstname Lastname, "Title of Article," *Title of Newspaper*, Month Day, Year, URL/Database.	1. Ethan Martin, "Johnson Calls UK Crisis Talks as Sturgeon Says Another Scottish Independence Vote Is Inevitable," *Washington Post*, September 22, 2019, http://www.washingtonpost.com/world/scotland-independence/.
Shortened Note	#. Lastname, "Shortened Title of Article."	2. Martin, "Scottish Independence Vote."
Bibliography	Lastname, Firstname. "Title of Article." *Title of Newspaper*, Month Day, Year, page range. URL/Database.	Martin, Ethan. "Johnson Calls UK Crisis Talks as Sturgeon Says Another Scottish Independence Vote Is Inevitable." *Washington Post*, September 22, 2019. http://www.washingtonpost.com/world/scotland-independence/.

Online Article from a Library Database

	General Format	Example
Note: -Endnote -Footnote	#. Firstname Lastname, "Title of Article," *Title of Newspaper*, Month Day, Year, page, Database.	1. Leo Coleman, "A Visit to the Zoo," *Environmental Awareness*, July 30, 2019, B16, Free News Portal Plus.
Shortened Note	#. Lastname, "Shortened Title of Article," page.	2. Coleman, "Zoo," B19.
Bibliography	Lastname, Firstname. "Title of Article." *Title of Newspaper*, Month Day, Year, page range. Database.	Coleman, Leo. "A Visit to the Zoo." *Environmental Awareness*, July 30, 2019, B16–B19. Free News Portal Plus.

No Author (Special Case)

For newspaper article with no author:
- In notes, format the source as usually (omit the author and begin with the title of the article).
- In bibliography, **move the newspaper title into place of the author**.
- Remember to omit the initial article "The" from newspaper title:

	General Format	Example
Note: -Endnote -Footnote	#. "Title of Article," *Title of Newspaper*, Month Day, Year, page, URL/Database.	1. "Electoral Reforms in India," *Politics*, August 4, 2021, 17.
Shortened Note	#. "Shortened Title of Article," page.	2. "Electoral Reforms in India," 17.
Bibliography	*Title of Newspaper.* "Title of Article." Month Day, Year, page range. URL/Database.	*Politics.* "Electoral Reforms in India." August 4, 2021, 17–18.

News Services

- News services (the Associated Press, the United Press International, etc.) usually stand in place of the author:

	General Format	Example
Note: -Endnote -Footnote	#. News Service, "Title of Article," *Title of Newspaper*, Month Day, Year, page, URL/Database.	1. Associated Press, "A Drowning Tragedy," *Berkeley News*, July 14, 2018, http://www.berkeleynews.com/4473940.
Shortened Note	#. News Service, "Shortened Title of Article," page.	2. Associated Press, "Texas A&M Galveston Professor."
Bibliography	News Service. "Title of Article." *Title of Newspaper*, Month Day, Year, page range. URL/Database.	Associated Press. "A Drowning Tragedy." *Berkeley News*, July 14, 2018. http://www.berkeleynews.com/4473940.

Scholarly Journal Articles

les:
- Article titles are enclosed in double quotation marks.
- Journal titles are italicized:
  - Omit the initial article "The" from journal titles.

blication information:
- Follow the journal title with:
  - **Volume number**:
    - Do not use "vol.," simply provide the volume number.
    - Do not italicize.
  - **Issue number** separated from the volume with a comma:
    - Use abbreviation "no." before the issue number.
    - Do not italicize.

ate of publication:
- Always include the year of publication.
- Additionally, the month or season may be included.

age numbers:
- In notes, include the exact page number of the cited material.
- In bibliography, include the full page range of the article:
  - Do not include the full page range **if the article is interrupted** by much-unrelated information.
- For online articles with no available pages, simply omit pages (do not include any other locator):

	General Format	Example
Note: -Endnote -Footnote	#. Firstname Lastname, "Title of Article," *Title of Journal* #volume, no. # (Month Year): page, DOI/Database/URL.	1. Aaliyah Thompson, "Writing and Performance as Path," *Social Action* 4, no. 14 (March 2020): 216, https://doi.org/10.1086/678242.
Shortened Note	#. Lastname, "Shortened Title of Article," page.	2. Thompson, "Writing and Performance," 219.
Bibliography	Lastname, Firstname. "Title of Article." *Title of Journal* #volume, no. # (Month Year): page range. DOI/Database/URL.	Thompson, Aaliyah. "Writing and Performance as Path." *Social Action* 4, no. 14 (March 2020): 210–23. https://doi.org/1049.5504.3332.

Different punctuation is used to separate publication information and page range:
- Use a colon only if the final publication information element is date or volume.
- Use a comma if the final publication information element is issue.

Publication Information	Volume, Issue, Date	Volume, No Issue, No Date	No Volume, Issue, No Date
General Format	*Journal Title* #volume, no. # (Month Year): page range.	*Journal Title* #volume: page range.	*Journal Title*, no. #, page range.
Example	*Critical Inquiry* 1, no. 3 (May 1975): 479–96.	*Social Networks* 14:213–29.	*Diogenes*, no. 25, 84–117.

Print Article

	General Format	Example
Note: -Endnote -Footnote	#. Firstname Lastname, "Title of Article," *Title of Journal* #volume, no. # (Month Year): page.	1. Jeremiah Collins, "Religion and Psychology," *Science* 34, no. 4 (April 2019): 321–29.
Shortened Note	#. Lastname, "Shortened Title of Article," page.	2. Collins, "Religion and Psychology," 329.
Bibliography	Lastname, Firstname. "Title of Article." *Title of Journal* #volume, no. # (Month Year): page range.	Collins, Jeremiah. "Religion and Psychology." *Science* 34, no. 4 (April 2019): 321–35.

Online Articles

For online article:
1. Include DOI.
2. If no DOI is available, include the library database name.
3. If the article is not from a library database, include URL.

Access dates are usually not required, however, if instructed:
- Include access date before DOI / Database / URL.

Online Article from the Internet (with URL)

	General Format	Example
Note: -Endnote -Footnote	#. Firstname Lastname, "Title of Article," *Title of Journal* #volume, no. # (Month Year): page, accessed Month Day, Year, URL.	1. Abigail Jenkins, "The Impact of Contraceptive Access on High School Graduation," *Science Advances* 56, no. 2 (April 2018): 65, accessed September 2, 2021, https://advances.sciencej.org/content/7/19/eabf6732
Shortened Note	#. Lastname, "Shortened Title of Article," page.	2. Jenkins, "Impact of Contraceptive Access," 68.
Bibliography	Lastname, Firstname. "Title of Article." *Title of Journal* #volume, no. # (Month Year): page range. Accessed Month Day, Year. URL.	Jenkins, Abigail. "The Impact of Contraceptive Access on High School Graduation." *Science Advances* 56, no. 2 (April 2018): 60–69. Accessed September 2, 2021. https://advances.sciencej.org/content/7/19/eabf6732.

Online Article from the Internet (with DOI)

	General Format	Example
Note: -Endnote -Footnote	#. Firstname Lastname, "Title of Article," *Title of Journal* #volume, no. # (Month Year): page, DOI.	1. Natalie Stewart, "School Uniforms," *Nature Communications* 55, no. 7 (Winter 2020), 21, http://doi.org/1004.3548.5680/chkg77.
Shortened Note	#. Lastname, "Shortened Title of Article," page.	2. Stewart, "School Uniforms," 21.
Bibliography	Lastname, Firstname. "Title of Article." *Title of Journal* #volume, no. # (Month Year): page range. DOI.	Stewart, Natalie. "School Uniforms." *German Nature Communications* 55, no. 7 (Winter 2020): 21–23. http://doi.org/1004.3548.5680/chkg77.

Online Article from a Library Database

- For online article from a library database with no DOI, include the database rather than URL:

	General Format	Example
Note: -Endnote -Footnote	#. Firstname Lastname, "Title of Article," *Title of Journal* #volume, no. # (Month Year): page, Database.	1. Lincoln Perry, "Penmanship and Calligraphy Samples," *ELife* 49, no. 6 (October 2014): 44, WorldCat.
Shortened Note	#. Lastname, "Shortened Title of Article," page.	2. Perry, "Penmanship and Calligraphy Samples," 46.
Bibliography	Lastname, Firstname. "Title of Article." *Title of Journal* #volume, no. # (Month Year): page range. Database.	Perry, Lincoln. "Penmanship and Calligraphy Samples." *ELife* 49, no. 6 (October 2014): 44–49. WorldCat.

When citing reviews:
- Begin the entry with the author of the review and the title of the review (if there is any).
- Include the title of the reviewed work and its author (or any other contributors).
- Include the periodical title and publication information where the review is published.

For the review with no author:
- In bibliography, move the periodical title into place of the author.

Review of Book

	General Format	Example
Note: -Endnote -Footnote	#. Review-Author's Firstname Lastname, review of *Title of Book*, by Book-Author's Firstname Lastname, *Title of Journal* #volume, no. # (Month Year): page, DOI/Database/URL.	1. Cora Martinez, review of *Importance of Sleep*, by Matthew Powell, *International Journal of Medical Physics* 31, no. 5 (July 2003): 245, https://doi.org/1044.0685.97.6888.
	#. Review-Author's Firstname Lastname, "Title of Review," review of *Title of Book*, by Book-Author's Firstname Lastname, *Title of Magazine/Newspaper*, Month Day, Year, section, page, DOI/Database/URL.	2. Emily Sanchez, "Agricultural Chemistry and Environment," review of *Green and Sustainable Chemistry*, by Henry Simmons, *Journal of Biophysical Chemistry*, July 6, 2021, Reviews, http://www.bpcjournal.com/reviews/348267.
Shortened Note	#. Review-Author's Lastname, review of *Shortened Title of Book*, page.	3. Martinez, review of *Importance of Sleep*, 245. 4. Sanchez, review of *Green and Sustainable Chemistry*.
Bibliography	Review-Author's Lastname, Firstname. Review of *Title of Book*, by Book-Author's Firstname Lastname. *Title of Journal* #volume, no. # (Month Year): page range. DOI/Database/URL. Review-Author's Lastname, Firstname. "Title of Review." Review of *Title of Book*, by Book-Author's Firstname Lastname. *Title of Magazine/Newspaper*, Month Day, Year, section, page range. DOI/Database/URL.	Martinez, Cora. Review of *Importance of Sleep*, by Matthew Powell. *International Journal of Medical Physics* 31, no. 5 (July 2003): 234–45. https://doi.org/1044.0685.97.6888. Sanchez, Emily. "Agricultural Chemistry and Environment." Review of *Green and Sustainable Chemistry*, by Henry Simmons. *Journal of Biophysical Chemistry*, July 6, 2021, Reviews. http://www.bpcjournal.com/reviews/348267.

Review of Play / Film / Concert

	General Format	Example
Note: -Endnote -Footnote	#. Review-Author's Firstname Lastname, "Title of Review," review of *Title of Artwork*, created by Creator's Firstname Lastname, *Title of Magazine/Newspaper*, Month Day, Year, page, DOI/Database/URL.	1. Henry Powell, "Save Water Save Earth," review of *Brave New World*, created by Eleanor Reed, *Signs*, April 9, 2017, http://www.signsog.com/2017/4/9/save_water.
Shortened Note	#. Review-Author's Lastname, review of *Shortened Title of Artwork*, page.	2. Powell, review of *Brave New World*.
Bibliography	Review-Author's Lastname, Firstname. "Title of Review." Review of *Title of Artwork*, created by Creator's Firstname Lastname. *Title of Magazine/Newspaper*, Month Day, Year, page range. DOI/Database/URL.	Powell, Henry. "Save Water Save Earth." Review of *Brave New World*, created by Eleanor Reed. *Signs*, April 9, 2017. http://www.signsog.com/2017/4/9/save_water.

5.4 Reference Books: Encyclopedias, Dictionaries, Guides, etc.

General Guidelines

Reference books are usually arranged alphabetically or organized into sections:
- For reference books organized into alphabetical entries (encyclopedias, dictionaries, etc.):
  - **Cite by specific entry** preceded by "s.v." (from Latin "under the word") or "s.vv." (for plural).
- For reference books organized into sections (guides, manuals, etc.):
  - **Cite by specific section number** (for example, 11.329–30).

Widely Known Reference Books

Widely known reference books (Oxford English Dictionary, Wikipedia, etc.) are usually cited in notes only:
- Include the edition number and the year of publication:
  - Other publication information **may be omitted**.
- For online reference books, include revision date or an access date:

	General Format	Example
Note: -Endnote -Footnote	#. Author's Firstname Lastname (if available), *Reference Work Title*, # ed. (Year), s.v. "entry," last updated/accessed Month Day, Year, URL.	1. *Macmillan Essential Dictionary*, 8th ed. (1999), s.v. "depression." 2. *Collins English Dictionary*, 13th ed. (2013), s.vv. "doctor," "nurse." 3. Emilia Long, *Concise English Dictionary*, 3rd ed. (2019), s.v. "gravity," accessed August 28, 2021, https://www.concisedictionaryeng.com/23567 4. *Merriam-Webster*, s.v. "gratitude (*n.*)," accessed August 28, 2021, https://www.merriam-webster.com/dictionary/gratitude.

Little-Known Reference Books

Little-known reference books are cited both in notes and bibliography:
- Include the full publication information:
  - Format the entries as any other publication of that medium (usually **as books**):

	General Format	Example
Note: -Endnote -Footnote	#. Editor's Firstname Lastname, ed., *Reference Work Title* (City: Publisher, Year), s.v. "entry." #. *Title: Subtitle* (City: Publisher, Year), location.	1. Jaxon Morris, ed., *Century Dictionary* (Haven, CT: Century Press, 2013), s.v. "postpartum depression." 2. *The AIIO Style Manual* (New York: AIIO Press, 2019), 11.332.
Shortened Note	#. Editor's Lastname, *Shortened Reference Work Title*, s.v. "word." #. *Shortened Title*, location.	3. Morris, *Century Dictionary*, s.v. "postpartum depression." 4. *AIIO Style Manual*, 11.332.
Bibliography	Editor's Lastname, Firstname, ed. *Reference Work Title*. City: Publisher, Year. *Title: Subtitle*. City: Publisher, Year.	Morris, Jaxon, ed. *Century Dictionary*. Haven, CT: Century Press, 2013. *The AIIO Style Manual*. New York: AIIO Press, 2019.

Online Reference Works with No Print Version / Wikipedia

Treat an online reference work with no print version (for example, Wikipedia) **as a website**:
- Do not italicize the title of such an online reference work.
- A time stamp may be included.

Remember that Wikipedia is generally not considered a valid source for academic papers.

	General Format	Example
Note: -Endnote -Footnote	#. Online Reference Work Title, s.v. "entry," updated/last modified/accessed Month Day, Year, hh:mm, URL.	1. Wikipedia, s.v. "Tom Cruise," last modified August 20, 2021, 14:40, https://en.wikipedia.org/wiki/Tom_Cruise.

5.5 Websites

General Guidelines

Remember that information available on the internet is generally not considered a reliable source for academic papers:
- It is usually **enough to describe webpage content in the text** without a formal citation.
- If instructed to use citations, websites are normally cited in notes and are not included in bibliography.

Titles:
- Titles of web pages, headers, blog posts are enclosed in double quotation marks.
- Titles of websites are neither italicized, nor enclosed in double quotation marks.
- Titles of blogs are italicized.
- When in doubt whether to use regular or italicized font, **regular font is the safer choice**.
- For the web page with no title, use a description of the site with the word "website" in parentheses.

Dates:
- Include publication date, date of revision / update / edition / modification:
  - Use respective phrase to distinguish: Published / Updated / Last modified.
- If no date is available, include an access date instead.

Pay attention: Online periodicals (newspapers and magazines) are treated as periodicals, **NOT** as websites.

Web Page with Author

	General Format	Example
Note: -Endnote -Footnote	#. Firstname Lastname, "Title of Web Page" / Description of Web Page (website), Title of Website / Description of Website, Owner, updated/last modified/accessed Month Day, Year, URL.	1. Angel Robinson, "Disaster Management," ManagementTeo, accessed August 23, 2021, http://www.management.teo.com/art/5363457/.
Shortened Note	#. Lastname, "Shortened Title of Web Page" / Shortened Description of Web Page.	2. Robinson, "Disaster Management."
Bibliography	Lastname, Firstname. "Title of Web Page" / Description of Web Page (website). Title of Website / Description of Website, Owner. Updated/Last modified/Accessed Month Day, Year. URL.	Robinson, Angel. "Disaster Management." ManagementTeo. Accessed August 23, 2021. http://www.management.teo.com/art/536345 7/.

Web Page with No Author

For a web page with no clear author:
- In notes, begin the entry with the title.
- In bibliography, **move the owner of the website** (association, corporation, etc.) into place of the author:

	General Format	Example
Note: -Endnote -Footnote	#. "Title of Web Page" / Description of Web Page (website), Title of Website / Description of Website, Owner, updated/last modified/accessed Month Day, Year, URL.	1. "Free Grammar Software," Grammar Plus, WD Corporation, updated May 13, 2021, https://www.grammarplus.com/soft/free/09346. 2. "Liberty and Anarchy," East Delta University, accessed September 2, 2021, http://www.eastdelta.edu/. 3. Health and fitness (website), Editorium Education, accessed September 4, 2021, http://www.healfandfitness.edit.com/246534678.
Shortened Note	#. "Shortened Title of Web Page" / Shortened Description of Web Page.	4. "Free Grammar Software." 5. "Liberty and Anarchy." 6. Health and fitness.
Bibliography	Owner. "Title of Web Page" / Description of Web Page (website). Title of Website / Description of Website. Updated/Last modified/Accessed Month Day, Year. URL.	WD Corporation. "Free Grammar Software." Grammar Plus. Updated May 13, 2021. https://www.grammarplus.com/soft/free/09346. East Delta University. "Liberty and Anarchy." Accessed September 2, 2021. http://www.eastdelta.edu/. Editorium Education. Health and fitness (website). Accessed September 4, 2021. http://www.healfandfitness.edit.com/246534678.

Entire Website

	General Format	Example
Note: -Endnote -Footnote	#. Title of Website / Description of Website (website), Owner, updated/last modified/accessed Month Day, Year, URL.	1. Global Facilities, Orange Corporation, accessed March 18, 2021, https://www.globalfacilities.com. 2. Tourist guide to lake Oreo (website), CityOne Management, accessed March 18, 2021, http://www.lakeoreoguide.org.
Shortened Note	#. Shortened Title of Website / Shortened Description of Website.	3. Global Facilities. 4. Lake Oreo.
Bibliography	Owner. Title of Website / Description of Website (website). Updated/Last modified/Accessed Month Day, Year. URL.	Orange Corporation. Global Facilities. Accessed March 18, 2021. https://www.globalfacilities.com. CityOne Management. Tourist guide to lake Oreo (website). Accessed March 18, 2021. http://www.lakeoreoguide.org.

Blog Post

Generally, blog posts are cited only in notes and are not included in bibliography.

Blog posts are formatted as online newspaper articles:
- Titles of blog posts are enclosed in double quotation marks.
- Titles of blogs are italicized.
- The word "blog" is added after the title of blog in parentheses (**unless the word "blog" is already a part** of the title).
- If the blog is part of a larger publication (for example, a blog published through WordPress), include its title as well:

	General Format	Example
Note: -Endnote -Footnote	#. Firstname Lastname, "Title of Post," *Title of Blog* (blog), *Name of Larger Publication*, Month Day, Year, URL.	1. David Jackson, "Semantic Barriers in Peoples Communication English Language," *Communication Plus* (blog), *WordPress*, September 30, 2019, http://commplus.wordpress.com/articles/semantic_ba rriers/.
Shortened Note	#. Lastname, "Shortened Title of Post."	2. Jackson, "Semantic Barriers."
Bibliography	Lastname, Firstname. "Title of Post." *Title of Blog* (blog). *Name of Larger Publication*, Month Day, Year. URL.	Jackson, David. "Semantic Barriers in Peoples Communication English Language." *Communication Plus* (blog). *WordPress*, September 30, 2019. http://commplus.wordpress.com/articles/sem antic_barriers/.

Comment

When referring to specific comment to the source that has already been cited in paper (blog post, social media post, etc.):
- Comments are usually described in the text without a formal citation.
- If formal citation is needed:
  - List the name of commenter and the date.
  - Include the **related source** (blog post, social media post, etc.) – use a shortened form because it has already been cited in full.
  - **Do not include comment in bibliography** as long as the related source is already included in bibliography:

	General Format	Example
Note: -Endnote -Footnote	#. Name of Commenter, Month Day, Year, comment on [Source] / reply to … , URL.	1. Jacob, January 22, 2020, comment on Jackson, "Semantic Barriers," http://commplus.wordpress.com/articles/semantic_b arriers/comment_8566786578. 2. Everly, January 25, 2020, reply to Jacob, http://commplus.wordpress.com/articles/semantic_b arriers/comment_8566789534.

5.6 Social Media

General Guidelines

It is usually enough to describe social media content in the text without a formal citation:
- If instructed to cite social media posts formally, notes may be used.
- For a continuously cited social media post, include it in bibliography.

Author:
- List the real name with a **screen name** in parentheses if known:
  o Use only a screen name in place of the author if the real name is not known.

Title:
- Use **up to 160 first characters** (including spaces) of the post in place of the title enclosed in double quotation marks:
  o Use original capitalization, spelling, punctuation, etc.
  o Cut the post off with an ellipsis if the limit of 160 characters is reached.

Keep in mind that only public content is treated as social media posts:
- For private content, treat it as personal communication.
- It is a good practice to take a screenshot to avoid so that future changes would not undermine your paper.

	General Format	Example
Note: -Endnote -Footnote	#. Firstname Lastname (@screen_name), "Quotation up to 160 first characters," Type of Post, Month Day, Year, hh:mm, URL.	1. Asher Rogers (@rogers_ash9), "Moving out feels pretty good," Instagram photo, July 3, 2021, https://instagram.com/p/CBBcdersAa_/.
Shortened Note	#. Lastname, "Shortened Quotation."	2. Rogers, "Moving."
Bibliography	Lastname, Firstname (@screen_name). "Quotation." Type of Post, Month Day, Year, hh:mm. URL.	Rogers, Asher (@rogers_ash9). "Moving out feels pretty good." Instagram photo, July 3, 2021. https://instagram.com/p/CBBcdersAa_/.

Facebook

	General Format	Example
Note: -Endnote -Footnote	#. Firstname Lastname (@screen_name), "Quotation," Type of Post, Month Day, Year, hh:mm, URL.	1. Elizabeth Rodriguez, "Cause Love's such an old fashioned word, and Love dares you to care for the people on the edge of the night," Facebook, May 19, 2020, http://www.facebook.com/356875478560/.
Shortened Note	#. Lastname, "Shortened Quotation."	2. Rodriguez, "Love dares you to care."
Bibliography	Lastname, Firstname (@screen_name). "Quotation." Type of Post, Month Day, Year, hh:mm. URL.	Rodriguez, Elizabeth. "Cause Love's such an old fashioned word, and Love dares you to care for the people on the edge of the night." Facebook, May 19, 2020. http://www.facebook.com/356875478560/.

Instagram

	General Format	Example
Note: -Endnote -Footnote	#. Firstname Lastname (@screen_name), "Quotation," Type of Post, Month Day, Year, hh:mm, URL.	1. Michael Reed (@michreed_off), "New cover if ready, guys," Instagram photo, July 30, 2021, https://www.instagram.com/p/sjHBdu_8GbdF.
Shortened Note	#. Lastname, "Shortened Quotation."	2. Reed, "New cover."
Bibliography	Lastname, Firstname (@screen_name). "Quotation." Type of Post, Month Day, Year, hh:mm. URL.	Reed, Michael (@michreed_off). "New cover if ready, guys." Instagram photo, July 30, 2021. https://www.instagram.com/p/sjHBdu_8GbdF.

Twitter

	General Format	Example
Note: -Endnote -Footnote	#. Firstname Lastname (@screen_name), "Quotation," Type of Post, Month Day, Year, hh:mm, URL.	1. Isla Lewis (@IslaLewis4), "Whenever possible, I contact my friends abroad," Twitter, December 5, 2017, 10:25 p.m., https://twitter.com/IslaLewis4/status/02597620675.
Shortened Note	#. Lastname, "Shortened Quotation."	2. Lewis, "Whenever possible."
Bibliography	Lastname, Firstname (@screen_name). "Quotation." Type of Post, Month Day, Year, hh:mm. URL.	Lewis, Isla (@IslaLewis4). "Whenever possible, I contact my friends abroad." Twitter, December 5, 2017, 10:25 p.m. https://twitter.com/IslaLewis4/status/025976 20675.

Forums

Forums citations are formatted similarly to social media:
- In place of the title use the title of the thread.
- Include the title of forum in addition to the title of website:

	General Format	Example
Note: -Endnote -Footnote	#. Firstname Lastname (@screen_name), "Thread Title," Title of Forum, Title of Website, Month Day, Year, URL.	1. Leah Hughes, reply to "Overcoming the Paradox of Choice," Modern Psycho, June 9, 2020, https://www.modernpsycho.com/thr/overcoming_par adaox_choice/.
Shortened Note	#. Lastname, "Shortened Thread Title."	2. Hughes, "Paradox of Choice."
Bibliography	Lastname, Firstname (@screen_name). "Thread Title." Title of Forum, Title of Website, Month Day, Year. URL.	Hughes, Leah. Reply to "Overcoming the Paradox of Choice." Modern Psycho, June 9, 2020. https://www.modernpsycho.com/thr/overco ming_paradaox_choice/.

Reddit

	General Format	Example
Note: -Endnote -Footnote	#. u/screen_name, "Thread Title," r/Title of Forum, Reddit, Month Day, Year, URL.	1. u/geoff967, "Traffic Problems," r/Driving, Reddit, October 7, 2017, https://www.reddit.com/r/Driving/comments/geoff96 7565/traffic_problems /.
Shortened Note	#. u/screen_name, "Shortened Thread Title."	2. u/geoff967, "Traffic Problems."
Bibliography	u/screen_name. "Thread Title." r/Title of Forum, Reddit, Month Day, Year. URL.	u/geoff967. "Traffic Problems." r/Driving, Reddit, October 7, 2017. https://www.reddit.com/r/Driving/comments /geoff967565/traffic_problems /.

Quora

	General Format	Example
Note: -Endnote -Footnote	#. Firstname Lastname, "Thread Title," Quora, Month Day, Year, URL.	1. Christopher Lewis, reply to "How can I develop self-confidence and self-esteem?," Quora, April 26, 2020, https://www.quora.com/How-can-I-develop-self-confidence-and-self-esteem.
Shortened Note	#. Lastname, "Shortened Thread Title."	2. Lewis, "Self-confidence and self-esteem."
Bibliography	Lastname, Firstname. "Thread Title." Quora, Month Day, Year. URL.	Lewis, Christopher. Reply to "How can I develop self-confidence and self-esteem?." Quora, April 26, 2020. https://www.quora.com/How-can-I-develop-self-confidence-and-self-esteem.

5.7 Audiovisual Multimedia

General Guidelines

- Use the name of the **primer contributor** (writer, director, composer, artist, etc.) as the author:
  - Follow the name with the title of contributor.
- Include the information about the work (where it has been published, recorded, etc.).
- Include the information about the publisher.
- Include the medium of the work and any other useful information.

Online Video from the Internet

	General Format	**Example**
Note: -Endnote -Footnote	#. Firstname Lastname, "Title of Video," *Periodical,* Recording Date, video, length, URL. #. Firstname Lastname, director, *Title of Video,* Publisher, Publication Year, length, *Online Publisher,* URL. #. "Title of Video," from a performance on *Title of Show* televised by Publisher on Month Day, Year, video, length, URL.	1. Claire Parker, "Johnson Calls UK Crisis Talks as Sturgeon Says Another Scottish Independence Vote Is Inevitable," *The Washington Post*, May 9, 2021, video, 3:30, http://www.washingtonpost.com/world/2021/05/09/scotland-independence/. 2. Easton Flores, director, *The Children of Morelia,* Hill Station Productions, 2018, 44:23, *Futuristics,* https://vid.futuristics.com/video/3574658. 3. "Importance of Sleep," from a performance on *Morning Show with Alice* televised by ADR on January 5, 2019, video, 4:23, http://www.watchmorningtv.com/aliceshow/video/2019/1/5/34867035.
Shortened Note	#. Lastname, "Shortened Title of Video." #. Lastname, *Shortened Title of Video.* #. "Shortened Title of Video."	4. Claire, "Scottish Independence." 5. Flores, *Children of Morelia.* 6. "Importance of Sleep."
Bibliography	Lastname, Firstname. "Title of Video." *Periodical,* Recording Date. Video, length. URL. Lastname, Firstname, director. *Title of Video.* Publisher, Publication Year, length. *Online Publisher.* URL. "Title of Video." From a performance on *Title of Show* televised by Publisher on Month Day, Year. Video, length. URL.	Parker, Claire. "Johnson Calls UK Crisis Talks as Sturgeon Says Another Scottish Independence Vote Is Inevitable." *The Washington Post*, May 9, 2021. Video, 3:30. http://www.washingtonpost.com/world/2021/05/09/scotland-independence/. Flores, Easton, director. *The Children of Morelia.* Hill Station Productions, 2018, 44:23. *Futuristics.* https://vid.futuristics.com/video/3574658. "Importance of Sleep." From a performance on *Morning Show with Alice* televised by ADR on January 5, 2019. Video, 4:23. http://www.watchmorningtv.com/aliceshow/video/2019/1/5/34867035.

YouTube

	General Format	Example
Note: -Endnote -Footnote	#. Firstname Lastname, "Title of Video," Publisher, Year, YouTube Video, length, URL.	1. Christian Walker, "Centralization and Decentralization," Politics and People, 2011, YouTube Video, 9:42, https://www.youtube.com/watch?v=dsUjd_jf8.
Shortened Note	#. Lastname, "Shortened Title of Video."	2. Walker, "Centralization and Decentralization."
Bibliography	Lastname, Firstname. "Title of Video." Publisher. Year. YouTube Video, length. URL.	Walker, Christian. "Centralization and Decentralization." Politics and People. 2011. YouTube Video, 9:42. https://www.youtube.com/watch?v=dsUjd_jf8.

Ted Talk

As long as Ted Talk video is a **recording of speech**:
- Include information about location and date the performance was recorded:

	General Format	Example
Note: -Endnote -Footnote	#. Firstname Lastname, "Title of Video," filmed Month Day, Year in City, TED video, length, URL.	1. Daniel Morgan, "Meet the Women Fighting," filmed June 9, 2021 in Newark, NJ, TED video, 16:33, https://www.ted.com/talks/gabriel_nelson_talks_about_women_fighting.
Shortened Note	#. Lastname, "Shortened Title of Video."	2. Morgan, "Meet the Women Fighting."
Bibliography	Lastname, Firstname. "Title of Video." Filmed Month Day, Year in City, TED video, length. URL.	Morgan, Daniel. "Meet the Women Fighting." Filmed June 9, 2021 in Newark, NJ. TED video, 16:33 https://www.ted.com/talks/gabriel_nelson_talks_about_women_fighting.

TV Series Episode

- TV series titles are italicized.
- Episode and scene titles are enclosed in double quotation marks:

	General Format	Example
Note: -Endnote -Footnote	#. *Title of TV Show*, season #, episode #, "Title of Episode," directed by Firstname Lastname, aired Month Day, Year, on Network, URL.	1. *The Elephant Tonight*, season 2, episode 5, "Victory Game," directed by Llewellyn Wells, aired January 4, 2000, on ABC, https://itunes.apple.com/ca/tv-season/id636845897?i=3920576.
Shortened Note	#. *Shortened Title of TV Show*.	2. *Elephant Tonight*.
Bibliography	Lastname, Firstname, dir. *Title of TV Show*. Season #, episode #, "Title of Episode." Aired Month Day, Year, on Network. URL.	Wells, Llewellyn, dir. *The Elephant Tonight*. Season 2, episode 5, "Victory Game." Aired January 4, 2000, on ABC. https://itunes.apple.com/ca/tv-season/id636845897?i=3920576.

Film / DVD

- Film titles are italicized.
- **Treat the screenwriter as the primary author:**
  - o Move any other contributor's name to place of the author for emphasis:
    - ▪ Follow the name with the title (director, writer, actor, etc.).
- Include the medium (DVD, Blu-Ray Disc, etc.):

	General Format	Example
Note: -Endnote -Footnote	#. Firstname Lastname, *Title of Film*, directed by Firstname Lastname (Release Year; City: Studio, Physical Copy Year), Medium, length.	1. Sadie Phillips, *Breakfast Club*, directed by Caleb Hall (2003; Menlo Park, CA: CCA, 2009), DVD.
	#. *Title of Film*, directed by Firstname Lastname (Release Year; City: Studio, Physical Copy Year), Medium, length.	2. *Deep Breathing*, directed by Julian Clark (2014; Culver City, CA: Sony Pictures, 2018), DVD, 103 min.
	#. Firstname Lastname, director, *Title of Film* (Release Year; City: Studio, Physical Copy Year), Medium, length.	3. Sarah Morgan, director, *Awakenings* (2009; Santa Monica, CA: Parkes productions, 2018), Blu-Ray Disc, 720p HD.
Shortened Note	#. Lastname, *Shortened Title of Film*.	4. Phillips, *Breakfast Club*. 5. *Deep Breathing*. 6. Morgan, *Awakenings*.
Bibliography	#. *Title of Film*. Directed by Firstname Lastname. Release Year. City: Studio, Physical Copy Year. Medium, length.	Phillips, Sadie. *Breakfast Club*. Directed by Caleb Hall. 2003. Menlo Park, CA: CCA, 2009. DVD.
	#. Lastname, Firstname. *Title of Film*. Directed by Firstname Lastname. Release Year. City: Studio, Physical Copy Year. Medium, length.	*Deep Breathing*. Directed by Julian Clark. 2014. Culver City, CA: Sony Pictures, 2018. DVD, 103 min.
	#. Lastname, Firstname, director. *Title of Film*. Release Year. City: Studio, Physical Copy Year. Medium, length.	Morgan, Sarah, director. *Awakenings*. 2009. Santa Monica, CA: Parkes productions, 2018. Blu-Ray Disc, 720p HD.

Film Scene

When citing specific film scene, the bibliography includes only the film title with no specific scene:
- Film titles are italicized.
- Scene titles are enclosed in double quotation marks:
  - o Use the **original scene titles** as they appear on the medium:

	General Format	Example
Note: -Endnote -Footnote	#. "Title of Scene," *Title of Film*, directed by Firstname Lastname (Release Year; City: Studio, Physical Copy Year), Medium.	1. "Marriage," *The House on Mango Street*, directed by Camila Turner (1989; Tustin, CA: TusOne Production, 2013), DVD.
Shortened Note	#. "Shortened Title of Scene."	2. "Marriage."
Bibliography	*Title of Film*. Directed by Firstname Lastname. Release Year. City: Studio, Physical Copy Year. Medium.	*The House on Mango Street*. Directed by Camila Turner. 1989. Tustin, CA: TusOne Production, 2013. DVD.

Audio from the Internet

- For a downloadable file, include the **format** of the file:

	General Format	Example
Note: -Endnote -Footnote	#. "Title of Audio," *Title of Collection*, Contributors, Location, Month Day, Year, length, Format, Database/URL.	1. "Spring," *Concerto No. 1 in E major, Op. 8*, performed by John Harrison (violin) with Wichita State University Chamber Players, Wiedemann Recital Hall, February 6, 2000, 2 min., 52 sec., OGG, https://commons.wikimedia.org/wiki/File:02_-_Vivaldi_Spring_mvt_2_Largo_-_John_Harrison_violin.ogg.
Shortened Note	#. "Shortened Title of Audio."	2. "Spring."
Bibliography	"Title of Audio." *Title of Collection*. Contributors, Location, Month Day, Year, length. Format, Database/URL.	"Spring," *Concerto No. 1 in E major, Op. 8*. Performed by John Harrison (violin) with Wichita State University Chamber Players, Wiedemann Recital Hall, February 6, 2000, 2 min., 52 sec. OGG, https://commons.wikimedia.org/wiki/File:02_-_Vivaldi_Spring_mvt_2_Largo_-_John_Harrison_violin.ogg.

Podcast

	General Format	Example
Note: -Endnote -Footnote	#. Podcast Host Firstname Lastname and Guest Firstname Lastname, "Title of Episode," Date Aired, in *Title of Podcast*, produced by Organization, podcast, MP3 audio, length, accessed Month Day, Year, URL.	1. Aubrey Washington and Miles Perry, "The Changes in the Ocean," April 14, 2017, in *Everyday Science*, produced by SV Audio, podcast, MP3 audio, 1:03:50, accessed August 29, 2021, https://sciencevoice.com/podcast/no_34962/.
Shortened Note	#. Podcast Host Lastname and Guest Lastname, "Shortened Title of Podcast."	2. Washington and Perry, "Changes in the Ocean."
Bibliography	Podcast Host Lastname, Firstname, and Guest Firstname Lastname. "Title of Episode." Produced by Organization. *Title of Podcast*. Date Aired. Podcast, MP3 audio, length. Accessed Month Day, Year. URL.	Washington, Aubrey, and Miles Perry. "The Changes in the Ocean." Produced by FD Audio. *Everyday Science*. April 14, 2017. Podcast, MP3 audio, 1:03:50. Accessed August 29, 2021. https://sciencevoice.com/podcast/no_34962/.

Song

- Omit the release year if it is the same as the recording date:

	General Format	Example
Note: -Endnote -Footnote	#. Performer Firstname Lastname, "Title of Song," Contributors, recorded Date, track # on *Title of Album*, Recording Company, Release Year, Medium.	1. Britney Spears, "Toxic," recorded 2003, track 6 on *In the Zone*, Jive, 2004, compact disc. 2. Madonna, vocalist, "Girl Gone Wild," by Benny Benassi, Alle Benassi, and Jenson Vaughan, recorded 2011, track 1 on *MDNA*, Interscope Records, 2012, vinyl LP.
Shortened Note	#. Performer Lastname, "Shortened Title of Song,"	4. Spears, "Toxic." 5. Madonna, "Girl Gone Wild."
Bibliography	Performer Lastname, Firstname. "Title of Song." Contributors, Recorded Date. Track # on *Title of Album*. Recording Company, Release Year, Medium.	Spears, Britney. "Toxic." Recorded 2003. Track 6 on *In the Zone*. Jive, 2004, compact disc. Madonna. "Girl Gone Wild." By Benny Benassi, Alle Benassi, and Jenson Vaughan. Recorded 2011. Track 1 on *MDNA*. Interscope Records, 2012, vinyl LP.

Image from the Internet / Visual Arts (Photograph, Painting, Sculpture, etc.)

It is usually enough to present visual arts (images, photographs, paintings, sculptures, etc.) in the text without a formal citation:
- If instructed to cite visual arts formally, follow the guidelines:
  o The title of the work is italicized.
  o Include the date of creation.
  o Include medium, dimensions, physical location, and other useful information.

Medium:
- Medium includes images, photographs, paintings (oil on canvas), sculptures (ivory), cartoons, graphs, etc.

Dimensions:
- Provide dimensions in both imperial and metric units:
  o Include the **units given by the publisher** followed by **conversion in parentheses**.

Physical location:
- Physical location includes publication, museum, private collection, etc.:

	General Format	Example
Note: -Endnote -Footnote	#. Firstname Lastname, *Title of Photograph*, Date Created, photograph, *Publisher*, Date Published. #. Firstname Lastname, *Title of Painting*, Date Created, medium, height x width (unit conversion), Location, City, URL. #. Firstname Lastname, *Title of Sculpture*, Date Created, medium, height x width x depth (unit conversion), Location, City, URL.	1. Luna Hall, *Ballet Girl*, August 1998, photograph, *Vogue*, cover, October 1998. 2. Pablo Picasso, *Guernica*, 1937, oil on canvas, 11.5 x 25.6 ft. (3.49 x 7.76 m), Museo Reina Sofia, Madrid, https://www.museoreinasofia.es/visita/tipos-visita/visita-comentada/guernica-historia-icono. 3. *Nefertiti Bust*, 1345 BCE, limestone and stucco, 49 x 24.5 x 35 cm (19.29 x 9.45 x 13.78 in.), Neues Museum, Berlin.
Shortened Note	#. Lastname, *Shortened Title of Artwork*.	4. Hall, *Ballet Girl*. 5. Picasso, *Guernica*. 6. *Nefertiti Bust*.
Bibliography	Lastname, Firstname. *Title of Photograph*. Date Created. Photograph. *Publisher*, Date Published. Lastname, Firstname. *Title of Painting*. Date Created. Medium, height x width (unit conversion). Location, City. URL. Lastname, Firstname. *Title of Sculpture*. Date Created. Medium, height x width x depth (unit conversion). Location, City. URL.	Hall, Luna. *Ballet Girl*. August 1998. Photograph. *Vogue*, cover, October 1998. Picasso, Pablo. *Guernica*. 1937. Oil on canvas, 11.5 x 25.6 ft. (3.49 x 7.76 m). Museo Reina Sofia, Madrid. https://www.museoreinasofia.es/visita/tipos-visita/visita-comentada/guernica-historia-icono. *Nefertiti Bust*. 1345 BCE. Limestone and stucco, 49 x 24.5 x 35 cm (19.29 x 9.45 x 13.78 in.). Neues Museum, Berlin.

Musical Scores

- Format published musical scores as books:

	General Format	Example
Note: -Endnote -Footnote	#. Firstname Lastname, *Title of Scores* (City: Publisher, Year).	1. Frederic Chopin, *The Ultimate Piano Collection* (New York: G. Schirmer, 2015).
Shortened Note	#. Lastname, *Shortened Title of Scores*.	2. Chopin, *The Ultimate Piano Collection*.
Bibliography	Lastname, Firstname. *Title of Scores*. City: Publisher, Year.	Chopin, Frederic. *The Ultimate Piano Collection*. New York: G. Schirmer, 2015.

Map

It is usually enough to present maps in the text without a formal citation:
- If instructed to cite visual arts formally, follow the guidelines:
  - Include the cartographer.
  - Title of the map is italicized:
    - Use a **description** (regular font) if no title is available.
  - Include the size and/or scale of the map.
  - Include the publication details:

	General Format	Example
Note: -Endnote -Footnote	#. Firstname Lastname, cartographer, *Title of Map*, Year Created, height x width, in *Title of Collection* (City: Publisher, Year), location. #. Satellite view of Location, Google Earth, accessed Month Day, Year, URL. #. Cartographer, *Title of Map*, Year Created, additional information, 1:# scale, Publisher, Collection, URL.	1. Willow Murphy, cartographer, *Europe Map*, 1734, 56 x 89 cm, in *Cartography* (Mahwah, NJ: Lawrence Erlbaum, 2020), fig. 44.5. 2. Satellite view of Miami, Google Earth, accessed August 25, 2021, https://www.google.com/maps/search/miami/@25.7823404,-80.3695452,47988m/data=!3m1!1e3. 3. US Geological Survey, *Indianapolis West*, 2008; repr., 2019, 1:25,000 scale, National Map, US Topo Collection, http://nationalmap.gov/.
Shortened Note	#. Lastname, *Shortened Title of Map*. #. Satellite view of Location. #. Cartographer, *Shortened Title of Map*.	4. Murphy, *Europe Map*. 5. Satellite view of Miami. 6. US Geological Survey, *Indianapolis West*.
Bibliography	Lastname, Firstname, cartographer. *Title of Map*. Year Created. height x width. In *Title of Collection*. City: Publisher, Year. Satellite view of Location. Google Earth. Accessed Month Day, Year. URL. Cartographer. *Title of Map*. Year Created. additional information, 1:# scale. Publisher, Collection. URL.	Murphy, Willow, cartographer. *Europe Map*. 1734. 56 x 89 cm. In *Cartography*. Mahwah, NJ: Lawrence Erlbaum, 2020. Satellite view of Miami. Google Earth. Accessed August 25, 2021. https://www.google.com/maps/search/miami/@25.7823404,-80.3695452,47988m/data=!3m1!1e3. US Geological Survey. *Indianapolis West*. 2008; repr., 2009. 1:25,000 scale. National Map, US Topo Collection. http://nationalmap.gov/.

Live Performances

As long as live performances **cannot be accessed by readers**, they do not need to be included bibliography:
- Include as much information in notes as possible:
  - Include detailed information of location where live performance took place and date.

Play

	General Format	Example
Note: -Endnote -Footnote	#. *Title of Play*, Contributors, Location, City, Month Day, Year.	1. *Well, That Happened*, music and lyrics by Ross Williams, dir. Addison Robinson, chor. Chloe Simmons, Olympia Theater, Miami, June 30, 2017.
Shortened Note	#. *Shortened Title of Play*.	2. *Well, That Happened.*

Concert

	General Format	Example
Note: -Endnote -Footnote	#. *Title of Concert*, feat. Title of Band, Location, City, Month Day, Year.	1. *Rammstein Tour*, feat. Rammstein, Olympiastadion, Berlin, June 4, 2022.
Shortened Note	#. *Shortened Title of Concert*.	2. *Rammstein Tour*.

5.8 Academic Sources

Thesis / Dissertation

Thesis and dissertation are formatted as "informally" published books:
- Titles of thesis and dissertation are enclosed in double quotation marks:

	General Format	Example
Note: -Endnote -Footnote	#. Firstname Lastname, "Title of Thesis/Dissertation" (thesis/dissertation, Institution, Year), page, URL.	1. Sofia Foster, "Effective Ways of Reducing Air Pollution" (PhD dissertation, University of Toronto, 2016), 22–23, http://search.proquest.com/docview/0783574542.
Shortened Note	#. Lastname, "Shortened Title of Thesis/Dissertation," page.	2. Foster, "Reducing Air Pollution," 27.
Bibliography	Lastname, Firstname. "Title of Thesis/Dissertation." Thesis/Dissertation, Institution, Year. URL.	Foster, Sofia. "Effective Ways of Reducing Air Pollution." PhD dissertation, University of Toronto, 2016. http://search.proquest.com/docview/0783574542.

Abstract

- To cite an abstract of thesis or dissertation, simply add "abstract" after the title:

	General Format	Example
Note: -Endnote -Footnote	#. Firstname Lastname, "Title of Thesis/Dissertation," abstract (thesis/dissertation, Institution, Year), page, URL.	1. Sofia Foster, "Effective Ways of Reducing Air Pollution," abstract (PhD dissertation, University of Toronto, 2016), 2, http://search.proquest.com/docview/0783574542.
Shortened Note	#. Lastname, "Shortened Title of Thesis/Dissertation," page.	2. Foster, "Reducing Air Pollution," 2.
Bibliography	Lastname, Firstname. "Title of Thesis/Dissertation." Abstract. Thesis/Dissertation, Institution, Year. URL.	Foster, Sofia. "Effective Ways of Reducing Air Pollution." Abstract. PhD dissertation, University of Toronto, 2016. http://search.proquest.com/docview/0783574542.

Class Lecture

Generally, it is better to **find the direct source** rather than cite lecture:
- Ask your lecturer for a bibliography list of the lecture to find the full sources.
- If citing class lecture is the only option, notes entries are usually sufficient.

Remember that only class lectures from the **same course that the paper is written for** are allowed.

Option 1

	General Format	Example
Note	#. Lecture, Month Day, Year.	1. Lecture, November 13, 2018.
Shortened Note	#. Lecture.	2. Lecture.

	General Format	Example
Note: -Endnote -Footnote	#. Lecturer Firstname Lastname, "Title of Lecture" (lecture, Institution, City, Month Day, Year).	1. Allison Rivera, "Nonviolence in Action" (lecture, Technical Education College, Colorado Springs, CO, May 20, 2019).
Shortened Note	#. Lecturer Lastname, "Shortened Title of Lecture."	2. Rivera, "Nonviolence in Action."
Bibliography	Lecturer Lastname, Firstname. "Title of Lecture." Lecture, Institution, City, Month Day, Year.	Rivera, Allison. "Nonviolence in Action." Lecture, Technical Education College, Colorado Springs, CO, May 20, 2019.

Recorded Lecture / Speech

	General Format	Example
Note: -Endnote -Footnote	#. Firstname Lastname, "Title of Lecture" lecture/speech, Location, Month Day, Year, City, format, length, URL.	1. Jameson Gonzales, "Effects of Social Networking Sites," speech, University of California, April 16, 2017, San Francisco, radio broadcast, MPEG copy, 1:15:22, https://www.universityofcalifornia.edu/executive/lect/nn=34965872.
Shortened Note	#. Lastname, "Shortened Title of Lecture."	2. Gonzales, "Social Networking Sites."
Bibliography	Lastname, Firstname. "Title of Lecture." Lecture/Speech, Location, City, Month Day, Year, City. Format, length. URL.	Gonzales, Jameson. "Effects of Social Networking Sites." Speech, University of California, April 16, 2017, San Francisco. Radio broadcast, MPEG copy, 1:15:22. https://www.universityofcalifornia.edu/executive/lect/nn=34965872.

Lectures, Papers, PowerPoint Presentations, Panels, and Posters Presented at Meetings / Symposiums / Conferences

	General Format	Example
Note: -Endnote -Footnote	#. Firstname Lastname, "Title of Lecture" (medium, Sponsorship, City, Month Day, Year), page, URL.	1. Avery Hernandez, "Evolution and Revolution: Solutions in Action" (presentation, Annual Conference on Education Abroad, Paris, December 3 – December 8, 2016), 4. 2. Sebastian Cooper, "The Civil Rights Movement and the Effects" (PowerPoint presentation, 25th Annual Meeting of the American Society of International Law, Menlo Park, CA, April 18, 2019), http://asilaw.org/meetings/25/presentation/23487/poster002.pdf.
Shortened Note	#. Lastname, "Shortened Title of Lecture," page.	3. Hernandez, "Evolution and Revolution," 6. 4. Cooper, "Civil Rights Movement."
Bibliography	Lastname, Firstname. "Title of Lecture." Medium presented at Sponsorship, City, Month Day, Year. URL.	Hernandez, Avery. "Evolution and Revolution: Solutions in Action." Paper presented at the Annual Conference on Education Abroad, Paris, December 3 – December 8, 2016. Cooper, Sebastian. "The Civil Rights Movement and the Effects." Poster presented at the 25th Annual Meeting of the American Society of International Law, Menlo Park, CA, April 18, 2019. http://asilaw.org/meetings/25/presentation/23487/poster002.pdf.

Archived Published Manuscript

Use the abbreviation:
- MS for a single manuscript.
- MSS for several manuscripts.
- TS for typescript (if needed to distinguish a typescript from a handwritten work):

	General Format	Example
Note: -Endnote -Footnote	#. Firstname Lastname, "Title of Manuscript" [Year], MS #, Collection, Library, City.	1. Lucy Bryant, "Beauty Definition" [1845] MS 4124, Foster Collection, Fairfax Branch Library Los Angeles.
Shortened Note	#. Lastname, "Shortened Title of Manuscript."	2. Bryant, "Beauty Definition."
Bibliography	Lastname, Firstname. "Title of Manuscript" [Year]. MS #, Collection, Library, City.	Bryant, Lucy. "Beauty Definition" [1845]. MS 4124 Foster Collection, Fairfax Branch Library, Los Angeles.

Archived Unpublished Manuscript / Letter

	General Format	Example
Note: -Endnote -Footnote	#. Lastname to Lastname, Month Day, Year, Letter.	1. Richardson to Lopez, November 4, 1993, Letter.
Bibliography	Lastname, Firstname. Letter from Firstname Lastname, affiliations to Firstname Lastname, affiliations, Month Day, Year. Accessed Month Day, Year. URL.	Richardson, Joshua. Letter from Joshua Richardson, CQW to David Lopez, DF, November 4, 1993. Accessed August 29, 2021. http://www.patrickun.edu/FH/cjf_94h7GtFB C-324.

Unarchived Unpublished Manuscript / Letter

- Replace location information with "private collection of … " or "in the author's possession":

	General Format	Example
Note: -Endnote -Footnote	#. Lastname to Lastname, Month Day, Year, Letter.	1. Collins to Campbell, September 1, 1985, Letter.
Bibliography	Lastname, Firstname. Letter from Firstname Lastname to Firstname Lastname, in the author's possession / private collection of Firstname Lastname, Month Day, Year.	Collins, Bella. Letter from Bella Collins to Christian Campbell, private collection of Noah Moore, March 4, 1944.

Working Paper

	General Format	Example
Note: -Endnote -Footnote	#. Firstname Lastname, "Title of Paper" (working paper, Archives, Faculty, Institution, City, Year).	1. Gianna Alexander, "Live Art: The Awakened Performer" (working paper, California Archives, Faculty of Art Education, Vreeland College of the Healing Arts, Camarillo, CA, 1993).
Shortened Note	#. Lastname, "Shortened Title of Paper."	2. Alexander, "Live Art."
Bibliography	Lastname, Firstname. "Title of Paper." Working paper, Archives, Faculty, Institution, City, Year.	Alexander, Gianna. "Live Art: The Awakened Performer." Working paper, California Archives, Faculty of Art Education, Vreeland College of the Healing Arts, Camarillo, CA, 1993.

Course Handout

	General Format	Example
Note: -Endnote -Footnote	#. Firstname Lastname, "Title of Course Handout" (course notes for Title of Course, Institution, City, Month Day, Year).	1. Nicholas Wright, "Interpersonal Communication Skills" (course notes for GHU 1101, Sierra College, Grass Valley, CA, February 28, 2018).
Shortened Note	#. Lastname, "Shortened Title of Course Handout."	2. Wright, "Interpersonal Communication Skills."
Bibliography	Lastname, Firstname. "Title of Course Notes." Course notes for Title of Course, Institution, City, Month Day, Year.	Wright, Nicholas. "Interpersonal Communication Skills." Course notes for GHU 1101, Sierra College, Grass Valley, CA, February 28, 2018.

Course Notes from Blackboard

	General Format	Example
Note: -Endnote -Footnote	#. Instructor Firstname Lastname, "Title of Course Notes" (course notes for Title of Course, Institution, City, Month Day, Year), Blackboard.	1. Mila Cox, "The Psychospiritual Context of Nature in Healing" (course notes for GHU 1101, Sierra College, Grass Valley, CA, May 14, 2018), Blackboard.
Shortened Note	#. Instructor Lastname, "Shortened Title of Course Notes."	2. Cox, "Psychospiritual Context."
Bibliography	Lastname, Firstname. "Title of Course Notes." Course notes for Title of Course, Institution, City, Month Day, Year. Blackboard.	Cox, Mila. "The Psychospiritual Context of Nature in Healing." Course notes for GHU 1101, Sierra College, Grass Valley, CA, May 14, 2018. Blackboard.

Course Pack

Generally, course packs include periodical articles and books that should be cited respectively.

Otherwise, treat the items within course packs as chapters of edited books:

- Use the name of **your instructor** or department **as the editor**.
- Use the bookstore as the publisher.
- Use the date course packs were issued as the date of publication:

	General Format	Example
Note: -Endnote -Footnote	#. Firstname Lastname, "Title of Item" in *Title of Course Packs,* ed. Instructor Firstname Lastname (City: Bookstore, Year), page.	1. Jack Howard, "Means for Autistic People to Reconnect with Their Bodies," in *GHU 1101: Deep Breathing,* ed. Mila Cox (Grass Valley, CA: Sierra College Bookstore, 2021), 36.
Shortened Note	#. Lastname, "Shortened Title of Item," page.	2. Howard, "Means for Autistic People," 39.
Bibliography	Lastname, Firstname. "Title of Item." In *Title of Course Packs,* edited by Instructor Firstname Lastname. City: Bookstore, Year.	Howard, Jack. "Means for Autistic People to Reconnect with Their Bodies." In *GHU 1101: Deep Breathing,* edited by Mila Cox. Grass Valley, CA: Sierra College Bookstore, 2021.

5.9 Personal Communications

General Guidelines

Personal communications include:
- Interviews conducted by yourself,
- Direct messages,
- Emails,
- Telephone conversations,
- Letters, etc.

As long as personal communication **cannot be accessed by readers**, it is only cited in notes and is not included in bibliography.

Keep in mind that published interviews are **NOT** considered personal communication.

Interview Conducted by Yourself

- Treat the name of the interviewed person as the author.
- For interviews with anonymous sources, use "Anonymous Informant #1":
  - Explain in text why the source is not named:

	General Format	Example
Note: -Endnote -Footnote	#. Interviewee Firstname Lastname, interview by author, Month Day, Year.	1. Audrey Russell, interview by author, April 17, 2021.
	#. Interviewee Firstname Lastname (affiliations) in discussion with the author, Month Day, Year.	2. Ezra Griffin (executive assistant, Customer Service, FFA) in discussion with the author, April 28, 2021.
Shortened Note	#. Interviewee Lastname, interview/discussion.	3. Russell, interview. 4. Griffin, discussion.

Personal Email

- Treat the name of the **sender** as the author:

	General Format	Example
Note: -Endnote -Footnote	#. Sender Firstname Lastname, email message to author, Month Day, Year.	1. Hudson Hayes, email message to author, July 2, 2021.
Shortened Note	#. Sender Lastname, email message.	2. Hayes, email message.

Personal Message

- Treat the name of the **sender** as the author:

	General Format	Example
Note: -Endnote -Footnote	#. Sender Firstname Lastname, Social Media message to author, Month Day, Year.	1. Samantha Smith, Facebook direct message to author, July 8, 2021.
Shortened Note	#. Sender Lastname, Social Media message.	2. Smith, Facebook message.

5.10 Interviews

Published interviews and interviews conducted by another person **are NOT considered personal communication**:
- As long as published interviews can be accessed by readers, they are included both in notes and bibliography.

Published Interviews

- Include the full citation of the publisher (book, periodical article, TV show, radio, etc.) where the interview is found.

Published Interview from Periodical

	General Format	Example
Note: -Endnote -Footnote	#. Interviewee Firstname Lastname, "Title of Interview," interview by Interviewer Firstname Lastname, *Title of Periodical*, Month Day, Year, edition, section, page, URL/Database.	1. Greyson Ward, "Greyson Ward: Value of Oxygen and Water," interview by Michael Jenkins, *Geoscience*, October 25, 2019, general edition, sec. H.
Shortened Note	#. Interviewee Lastname, "Shortened Title."	2. Ward, "Oxygen and Water."
Bibliography	Interviewee Lastname, Firstname. "Title of Interview." Interview by Interviewer Firstname Lastname. *Title of Periodical*, Month Day, Year, edition, section, page. URL/Database.	Ward, Greyson. "Greyson Ward: Value of Oxygen and Water." Interview by Michael Jenkins. *Geoscience*, October 25, 2019, general edition, sec. H.

Broadcast Interview from TV / Radio

	General Format	Example
Note: -Endnote -Footnote	#. Interviewee Firstname Lastname, interview by Interviewer Firstname Lastname, *Title of Program*, Publisher, Month Day, Year.	1. Bella Diaz, interview by Allison Rogers, *Walking Camel*, 91.7 CVD FM, January 11, 2012.
Shortened Note	#. Interviewee Lastname, interview.	2. Diaz, interview.
Bibliography	Interviewee Lastname Firstname. *Title of Program*. Interview by Interviewer Firstname Lastname. Publisher, Month Day, Year.	Diaz, Bella. *Walking Camel*. Interview by Allison Rogers. 91.7 CVD FM, January 11, 2012.

Interview Conducted by Another Person (Unpublished Transcript)

For a transcript or recording of unpublished interview conducted by another person:
- Include location where transcript or recording can be found:

	General Format	Example
Note: -Endnote -Footnote	#. Interviewee Firstname Lastname, interview by Interviewer Firstname Lastname, Month Day, Year, transcript, Location.	1. Serenity Hill, interview by Thomas Watson, August 2006, interview J32, transcript, Modern Interview Archive, National Library, Switzerland.
Shortened Note	#. Interviewee Lastname, interview.	2. Hill, interview.
Bibliography	Interviewee Lastname, Firstname. Interview by Interviewer Firstname Lastname, Month Day, Year, transcript, Location.	Hill, Serenity. Interview by Thomas Watson. August 2006, interview J32, transcript, Modern Interview Archive, National Library, Switzerland.

5.11 Government Publications

Generally, it is enough to include the government publication title in the text without a formal citation as long as the paper has a few citations.

For formal citations, format notes and bibliography entries for government publications as books:
- Treat the governmental agency (name of government, government division, subsidiary division) as the author:

	General Format	Example
Note: -Endnote -Footnote	#. Name of Government, Government Division, Subsidiary Division, *Title of Publication*, Publication # / #edition (City: Publisher, Year), page, URL.	1. Department of the Treasury, Internal Revenue Service, *Employer's Tax Guide*, Pub. 15 (Washington, DC: Government Printing Office, 2021). 2. National Energy Board, *Canadian Energy Overview 2012* (Calgary, Canada: National Energy Board, 2013), 8, https://publications.gc.ca/collections/collection_2013/one-neb/NE4-2-7-2013-eng.pdf. 3. Government of Canada, Standards Council of Canada, Canadian General Standards Board, *Organic Production Systems: Permitted Substances Lists*, 2nd ed. (Ottawa: Canadian General Standards Board, 2021), 12.
Shortened Note	#. Name of Government, Government Division, Subsidiary Division, *Shortened Title of Publication*, page.	4. Department of the Treasury, Internal Revenue Service, *Employer's Tax Guide*. 5. National Energy Board, *Canadian Energy*, 12. 6. Government of Canada, Standards Council of Canada, Canadian General Standards Board, *Organic Production Systems*, 14.
Bibliography	Name of Government. Government Division. Subsidiary Division. *Title of Publication*. Publication # / #edition. City: Publisher, Year. URL.	U.S. Department of the Treasury, Internal Revenue Service. *Employer's Tax Guide*. Pub. 15. Washington, DC: Government Printing Office, 2021. National Energy Board. *Canadian Energy Overview 2012*. Calgary, Canada: National Energy Board, 2013. https://publications.gc.ca/collections/collection_2013/one-neb/NE4-2-7-2013-eng.pdf. Government of Canada. Standards Council of Canada. Canadian General Standards Board. *Organic Production Systems: Permitted Substances Lists*. 2nd ed. Ottawa: Canadian General Standards Board, 2021.

5.12 Legal Sources

General Guidelines

Generally, it is enough to include the legal materials in the text without a formal citation as long as the paper has a few citations.

For legal sources, **to indicate the subsequent citation** from the same source, use *id.* (in italics) instead of "ibid." in notes.

Chicago style recommends using *The Bluebook* detailed style guide to cite legal sources:
- Below you will find the basic level of legal sources citations needed for students.

U.S. Constitution

U.S. Constitution is included in notes only:
- Cite constitutions by the title, article, section, and clause:
  - Abbreviate titles of constitutions.
- Use **Roman** numerals (I, II, III, …) for amendment (amend.) and article (art.).
- Use **Arabic** numerals (1, 2, 3, …) for section (§) and clause (cl.):

	General Format	Example
Note: -Endnote -Footnote	#. Constitution Title subdivision, subdivision. #. Constitution Title subdivision, subdivision (repealed Year). #. Constitution Title of Year, subdivision, subdivision (superseded Year).	1. U.S. Const. art. II, §1, cl. 3. 2. Ariz. Const. art. IV, §2. 3. U.S. Const. amend. XI (repealed 1933). 4. Ark. Const. of 1868, art. IV, §1 (superseded 1874).

Act / Statute / Law / Code

- It is usually sufficient to provide the title of the act and the year in the text with no formal citation.

	General Format	Example
Note: -Endnote -Footnote	#. Title of Act/Statute/Law/Code, Source § number (Year) (additional information).	1. Performance Appraisal Code, 5 U.S.C. ch. 43 §§4301–04 (2006). 2. Recreational Vessels, 46 U.S.C. ch. 43 §4305 (1971) (repealed 2021).

Bill / Resolution

- For bills passed in state legislative bodies, include the state.
- For shortened note, it is sufficient to include **document number only**:

	General Format	Example
Note: -Endnote -Footnote	#. Title of Act, Document Number, Legislative Body number, Session § number (State Year).	1. Breastfeeding Promotion Act, H.R. 2758, 112th Cong. § 2 (2011). 2. House Floor Amendment 2 to S.B. 195. 77th Leg., 2nd Sess. § 4 (N.C. 2021).
Shortened Note	#. State Document Number.	3. H.R. 2758. 4. N.C. S.B. 195.

Hearing

	General Format	Example
Note: -Endnote -Footnote	*#. Title: Hearing on Bill Before the Committee*, Session page (Year) (statement of Firstname Lastname, Affiliations).	1. *The Progress for Indian Tribes Act: Hearing on H.R. 2031 Before the Subcomm. on Indigenous Peoples of the United States*, 116th Cong. (2019–2020) (statement of Darryl LaCounte, Director of the Bureau of Indian Affairs, U.S. Department of the Interior)

Court Decision / Legal Case

- It is usually sufficient to provide the title of legal case in the text with no formal citation.
- If a formal citation is needed, use notes only:
  - For the first (full) note:
    - Do not italicize or enclose the case name in double quotation marks.
  - For shortened notes:
    - Shorten the case name:
      - Generally, do not shorten the case names to "United States" as long as many cases begin with "United States."
    - **Italicize the shortened case name.**
    - **Use "at"** before the page number.
  - Shorten the person names in cases to surname only.
  - To cite the whole case, provide the first page number that the case begins on (for example: 510):
    - When referring to a specific page, follow the first page number with a specific page number using a comma (for example: 510, 512).
- Abbreviate the names of courts:

	General Format	Example
Note: -Endnote -Footnote	#. Case Name, Number Volume first-page, specific-page (Court Year) (additional information).	1. United States v. Quinones, 136 F.3d 1293, 1295 (11th Cir. 1998) 2. United States v. General Motors Corp., 702 F. Supp. 133 (N.D. Tex. 1988) 3. Robertson v. Utah, 401 U.S. 5 (1968). 4. Katz v. Carte Blanche, 52 F.R.D. 510, 512 (W.D. Pa.1971) ("the questions of law or fact common to the members of the class predominate over any questions affecting only individual members").
Shortened Note	*#. Shortened Case Name*, Number Volume at specific-page. *#. Id.* at page.	5. *Quinones*, 136 F.3d at 1293. 6. *General Motors Corp.*, 702 F. Supp. at 133. 7. *Robertson*, 401 U.S. at 5. 8. *Katz*, 52 F.R.D. at 510. 9. *Id.* at 512.

Digital File from Library of Congress

	General Format	Example
Note: -Endnote -Footnote	#. Title of Document, Date, Manuscript/Papers, Division, Library of Congress, Washington, DC, URL.	1. Letterbook, June 24, 1775, George Washington Papers, Series 3: Varick Transcripts, 1775–1785, Library of Congress, Washington, DC, http://memory.loc.gov/ammem/gwhtml/gwseries5.html.

6.0 AD SYSTEM: IN-TEXT CITATIONS / REFERENCE LIST EXAMPLES

Reference list entries are formatted like the bibliography entries with the only difference:
- **The year of publication is the second element** (it is placed between the author and the title of source).

Below there are examples of the most commonly used sources cited in AD referencing system:
- For more sources and details on formatting, check chapter "5.0 NB SYSTEM" of this guide.

6.1 Authors

- In reference list, the first author's name is ALWAYS inverted (Lastname, Firstname):
  - Only the first author's name is inverted.
- All following authors' and other contributors' names appear in normal order (Firstname Lastname).

1 Author

	General Format	Example
In-text	… (Lastname Year, page).	… (Scott 2021, 26).
Reference	Lastname, Firstname. Year. *Title: Subtitle*. City: Publisher.	Scott, Bella. 2021. *Effects of Pollution.* New York: Columbia University Press.

2 Authors

	General Format	Example
In-text	… (Lastname and Lastname Year, page).	… (Torres and Williams 2018, 224).
Reference	Lastname, Firstname, and Firstname Lastname. Year. *Title: Subtitle*. City: Publisher.	Torres, Lucy, and Thomas Williams. 2018. *Effects of Social Networking Sites.* Cheshire, CT: Graphics Press.

3 Authors

	General Format	Example
In-text	… (Lastname, Lastname, and Lastname Year, page).	… (Johnson, Adams, and Gray 2019, 298).
Reference	Lastname, Firstname, Firstname Lastname, and Firstname Lastname. Year. *Title: Subtitle*. City: Publisher.	Johnson, Jack, Mateo Adams, and Adrian Gray. 2019. *The Civil Rights Movement and the Effects.* Boston: Addison-Wesley.

4–10 Authors

	General Format	Example
In-text	… (Lastname et al. Year, page).	… (Green et al. 2020, 85).
Reference	Lastname, Firstname, Firstname Lastname, […], Firstname Lastname, and Firstname Lastname. Year. *Title: Subtitle*. City: Publisher.	Green, Nova, Charles Miller, Sarah Carter, and Ian Brooks. 2020. *Causes and Effects of the Popularity of Fast Food Restaurants.* New York: Norton.

11+ Authors

	General Format	Example
In-text	… (Lastname et al. Year, page).	… (Peterson et al. 1999, 23).
Reference	Lastname1, Firstname1, Firstname2 Lastname2, Firstname3 Lastname3, Firstname4 Lastname4, Firstname5 Lastname5, Firstname6 Lastname6, and Firstname7 Lastname7, et al. Year. *Title: Subtitle*. City: Publisher.	Peterson, Penelope, Samuel Perez, Brooklyn Price, Caleb Wood, Axel Parker, Matthew Powell, Chloe Cook, et al. 1999. *Animal Characteristics in People.* Melbourne: Cambridge University Press.

6.2 Books

Book

	General Format	Example
In-text	… (Lastname Year, page).	… (Edwards 2014, 76).
Reference	Lastname, Firstname. Year. *Title: Subtitle.* City: Publisher.	Edwards, Joseph. 2014. *Annoying Commercials.* New York: John Wiley.

Book (Edition Other Than the First)

	General Format	Example
In-text	… (Lastname Year, page).	… (Coleman 2019, 227).
Reference	Lastname, Firstname. Year. *Title: Subtitle.* # ed. City: Publisher.	Coleman, Savannah. 2019. *Ghosts and Goblins.* 3rd ed. New York: W. W. Norton.

Book (Edited / Translated)

Option 1 (Preferred)

	General Format	Example
In-text	… (Lastname Year, page).	… (Thompson 1998, 194).
Reference	Lastname, Firstname. Year. *Title: Subtitle.* Edited/Translated by Firstname Lastname. City: Publisher.	Thompson, Ryan. 1998. *Causes of the Great Depression.* Translated by Edith Grossman. Alexandria, VA: EEI Press.

Option 2 (Emphasize Contributors)

	General Format	Example
In-text	… (Lastname Year, page).	… (Reed 2018, 590).
Reference	Lastname, Firstname, ed./eds. Year. *Title: Subtitle.* City: Publisher.	Reed, Jaxson, ed. 2018. *Home, Sweet Home.* Melbourne: Cambridge University Press.

Introduction / Preface / Afterword in a Book

	General Format	Example
In-text	… (Lastname Year, page).	… (Morgan 1994, 23).
Reference	Lastname, Firstname. Year. Introduction to *Title: Subtitle,* by Firstname Lastname, pages. City: Publisher.	Morgan, Victoria. 1994. Introduction to *Five Things I Love the Most,* by Andrew Parker, xii–xxvii. London: Cape.

Chapter in a Book

	General Format	Example
In-text	… (Lastname Year, page).	… (Patterson 2014, 66).
Reference	Lastname, Firstname. Year. "Title of Chapter." In *Title of Book*, edited by Editor Firstname Lastname, pages. City: Publisher.	Patterson, Eva. 2014. "The Day Before an Examination." In *My School Life*, edited by Elizabeth Moore, 49–82. Haven, CT: Yale University Press.

E-Book

	General Format	Example
In-text	… (Lastname Year, page).	… (Stewart 2001, 186).
Reference	Lastname, Firstname. Year. *Title: Subtitle.* City: Publisher. DOI/URL/Database.	Stewart, Adam. 2001. *School's Surroundings and Examinations.* New York: Springer-Verlag. EBSCOhost.

6.3 Articles in Periodicals

- If the date of publication includes "Month Day, Year," **include it** in the reference entry to avoid ambiguity (even though **the year is repeated twice** in this case).

Magazine Article

	General Format	Example
In-text	… (Lastname Year, page).	… (Rivera 2003, 14).
Reference	Lastname, Firstname. Year. "Title of Article." *Title of Magazine*, Month Day, Year, page. URL.	Rivera, Dominic. 2003. "Learning to Play Piano." *Cornell Alumni Magazine*, January 2003, 14. http://www.cornellall.com/article-149384/.

Newspaper Article

	General Format	Example
In-text	… (Lastname Year, page).	… (Young 2005).
Reference	Lastname, Firstname. Year. "Title of Article." *Title of Newspaper*, Month Day, Year, edition, section, page. URL.	Young, Piper. 2005. "Healing the Mind Body Split." *Cherokee Phoenix*, September 14, 2005, Advice. http://www.cherokeeph.com/advice/healing-the-mind-body-split.

Newspaper Article (No Author)

For newspaper article with no author, **move the newspaper title** into place of the author:
- Remember to omit the initial article "The" from newspaper title:

	General Format	Example
In-text	… (*Title of Newspaper* Year, page).	… (*Chicago Tribune* 2020).
Reference	*Title of Newspaper*. Year. "Title of Article." Month Day, Year, edition, section, page. URL.	*Chicago Tribune*. 2020. "Live Art: The Awakened Performer." August 12, 2020.

Scholarly Journal Article

	General Format	Example
In-text	… (Lastname Year, page).	… (Murphy 2021, 220). … (Simmons 2013, 126).
Reference	Lastname, Firstname. Year. "Title of Article." *Title of Journal* #volume, no. # (Month or Season): page. DOI/URL.	Murphy, Claire. 2021. "Importance of Family." *Nature Communications* 15, no. 4 (Summer): 209–59. http://doi.org/10.9455/1163.
	Lastname, Firstname. Year. "Title of Article." *Title of Journal* #volume (#issue): page. DOI/URL.	Simmons, Nathan. 2013. "Copying in the Examination." *Journal of Measurement and Visualization* 65 (9): 126.

6.4 Reference Books: Encyclopedias and Dictionaries

- Widely known reference books (Oxford English Dictionary, Wikipedia, etc.) are usually cited in text only.
- **Do not italicize** the title of online reference work with no print version (for example, Wikipedia):

General Format		Example
In-text	… (*Reference Work Title*, # ed. (Year), s.v. "entry").	… (*Macmillan Essential Dictionary*, 2nd ed. (2009), s.v. "postpartum depression").
	… (Reference Work Title, s.v. "entry," updated/last modified/accessed Month Day, Year, URL).	… (Wikipedia, s.v. "Tom Cruise," last modified August 20, 2021, https://en.wikipedia.org/wiki/Tom_Cruise).

- Format citations of little-known reference works as books:

General Format		Example
In-text	… (Lastname Year, s.v. "entry").	… (Richardson 2018, s.v. "manic depression").
Reference	Lastname, Firstname. Year. *Reference Work Title*. City: Publisher.	Richardson, Sophie, ed. 2018. *Century Dictionary*. Miami: Hansen Books.

6.5 Websites

Web Page

General Format		Example
In-text	… (Lastname Year). … (Owner Year).	… (Wilson 2000). … (Orange Corporation 2005). … (CityOne Management n.d.).
Reference	Lastname, Firstname. Year. "Title of Web Page" / Description of Web Page (website). Title of Website / Description of Website, Owner. Updated/Last modified/Accessed Month Day, Year. URL. Owner. Year. "Title of Web Page" / Description of Web Page (website). Title of Website / Description of Website. Updated/Last modified/Accessed Month Day, Year. URL.	Wilson, Leonardo. 2000. "Disaster Management." ManagementTeo. Last modified February 11, 2000. http://www.management.teo.com/art/339278. Orange Corporation. 2005. "Sports and Games." Global Facilities. Updated January 19, 2005. https://www.globalfacilities.com/ar/f_93hf832. CityOne Management. n.d. Tourist guide to lake Oreo (website). Accessed March 18, 2021. http://www.lakeoreoguide.org/.

Blog Post

General Format		Example
In-text	… (Lastname Year).	… (Jackson 2019).
Reference	Lastname, Firstname. Year. "Title of Post." *Title of Blog* (blog), *Name of Larger Publication*. Month Day, Year. URL.	Jackson, David. 2019. "Semantic Barriers in Peoples Communication English Language." *Communication Plus* (blog), *WordPress*. September 30, 2019. http://commplus.wordpress.com/articles/semantic_barriers/.

6.6 Social Media

	General Format	Example
In-text	… (Lastname Year).	… (Lewis 2017).
Reference	Lastname, Firstname (@screen_name). Year. "Quotation up to 160 first characters." Type of Post, Month Day, Year, hh:mm. URL.	Lewis, Isla (@IslaLewis4). 2017. "Whenever possible, I contact my friends abroad." Twitter, December 5, 2017, 10:25 p.m. https://twitter.com/IslaLewis4/status/02597620675.

6.7 Audiovisual Multimedia

Online Video / YouTube

	General Format	Example
In-text	… (Lastname Year).	… (Walker 2011).
Reference	Lastname, Firstname. Year. "Title of Video." Publisher. YouTube Video, length. URL.	Walker, Christian. 2011. "Centralization and Decentralization." Politics and People. YouTube Video, 9:42. https://www.youtube.com/watch?v=dsUjd_jf8.

Film / TV Series

	General Format	Example
In-text	… (Lastname Year).	… (Phillips 2003). … (Edwards 1989).
Reference	Lastname, Firstname. Year. *Title of Film*. Directed by Firstname Lastname. City: Studio. DVD Lastname, Firstname. Year. "Title of Episode." *Title of Series*. Directed by Firstname Lastname. City: Studio. DVD.	Phillips, Sadie. 2003. *Breakfast Club*. Directed by Caleb Hall. Menlo Park, CA: CCA. DVD. Edwards, Luca. 1989. "Marriage." *The House on Mango Street*. Directed by Camila Turner. Tustin, CA: TusOne Production. DVD.

6.8 Academic Sources

Lectures and Papers Presented at Conference

	General Format	Example
In-text	… (Lastname Year, page).	… (Taylor 2008).
Reference	Lastname, Firstname. Year. "Title of Work." Medium presented at Sponsorship, City, Month Day, Year. URL.	Taylor, Grace. 2008. "Disadvantages and Advantages of Mobile Phones." Presentation at the annual conference of GRAMVILL, Gaithersburg, MD, October 22–24. http://www.gramconference.org/2008/disadvantages-and-advantages-of-mobile-phones.

Unpublished Manuscript

	General Format	Example
In-text	… (Lastname Year, page).	… (Williams 2021, 4).
Reference	Lastname, Firstname. Year. "Title of Work." *Title of Series*. Organization, Month Day, Year. URL.	Williams, John. 2021. "Causes of Global Warming." *History of Global Warming*. Center of Education, Columbia University, May 13, 2021. http://www.columbiau.edu/education/works/causes-of-global-warming.pdf.

7.0 CHICAGO SAMPLE PAPER

For the purpose of demonstrating a general layout and common formatting
(such as formatting of footnotes, bibliography, title page, contents, abstract, headings, lists, tables and illustrations, quotations, etc.),
the following Chicago sample paper contains "Lorem ipsum" filler text to emphasize the style elements over content.

SOCIAL ACTION:

WRITING AND PERFORMANCE AS PATH

Oliver Johnson

Sociology 224: Sociology, Social Psychology

September 16, 2021

Contents

Abstract

Lorem ipsum dolor sit amet, consectetur adipiscing elit. Sed pretium ante eu eros semper scelerisque. Integer at convallis nibh. Fusce efficitur felis vel felis pulvinar aliquam. Duis bibendum aliquet dignissim. Cras urna nisi, feugiat at sem sit amet, consequat tristique urna. In eleifend semper gravida. Aenean vehicula, ex eu tincidunt commodo, elit dolor placerat eros, non ornare neque ipsum nec leo. Proin condimentum finibus arcu eget mollis. In sagittis nulla at mollis lacinia. Nunc eleifend ante eu lobortis viverra. Curabitur varius risus vel nunc vehicula ultrices. Mauris turpis massa, sollicitudin sit amet ornare ac, pharetra sed velit. Maecenas auctor sapien id turpis varius rhoncus. Ut mollis arcu at fermentum pulvinar. Duis a libero ac ligula ullamcorper aliquam vehicula eget nulla. Donec eget orci vitae metus commodo malesuada eu a metus. Sed lacinia eros sed mauris dignissim malesuada. Proin a eros ullamcorper, porta ex ac, ultricies ligula. Suspendisse potenti. Sed erat lacus, dapibus a mauris non, congue volutpat diam. Curabitur eget metus blandit, gravida arcu vel, placerat est. Donec eleifend, nibh ullamcorper vehicula finibus, velit ex dapibus odio, in faucibus velit nibh non tellus. Proin auctor magna id diam dignissim, a finibus ipsum eleifend. Morbi at lacinia felis. Cras imperdiet, ex.

Keywords: Ipsum, purus, pulvinar, porttitor, consectetur

Global Pollution

Lorem ipsum dolor sit amet, consectetur adipiscing elit. Sed ut ex convallis magna facilisis pellentesque. Nunc auctor tellus velit, vitae tempor nisl hendrerit eget. Nulla facilisi. "Nulla vestibulum eget risus sit amet aliquam."[1] Aliquam consequat luctus erat, sed faucibus nulla dapibus nec. Fusce a arcu et dolor pulvinar vestibulum. Nunc sit amet justo vehicula, imperdiet neque id, ultricies mi. Accessibility and convenience include (*a*) the broad variety of products and services, (*b*) online comparison, (*c*) adequate buildings, (*d*) basic and urban infrastructure services.

Environment

Maecenas erat odio, pharetra non lectus eget, fermentum viverra felis. Praesent auctor iaculis quam et posuere. Proin aliquet hendrerit mi quis ullamcorper.[2] In porttitor felis sed ex egestas, ut scelerisque dolor consequat. Sed sed lacus mauris. Vestibulum maximus eros enim, in vehicula lacus fringilla eu. Nunc feugiat lectus non dolor dignissim, dignissim blandit nibh pretium. Mauris ultrices, ante ut efficitur vehicula, quam tortor pellentesque erat, eget venenatis risus velit ornare tortor. There are two parts to referencing for each system:

1. The citations within the text of your paper
    1.1. Notes
    1.2. Parenthetical citations
2. An alphabetical list of sources at the end of your paper
    2.1. Bibliography
    2.2. References

Donec ac nisi ornare, viverra tellus at, lobortis est. Sed malesuada maximus felis, at ultricies neque commodo et. Vivamus consequat dolor "eros."[3]

---

1. James Brooks, *Favorite Athlete* (New York: Pocket Books, 2018), 43.

2. Mason White, "Nonviolence in Action," *Peace Studies*, March 2020, 49.

3. Brooks, *Favorite Athlete*, 64.

Wildlife

Mauris ullamcorper commodo magna, non tincidunt urna feugiat vel. Nulla malesuada sem a enim efficitur luctus, id rutrum justo dapibus eget. Integer tempus et orci ut rutrum reported that

- the company will be launched in 2022;
- the director position is still open; and
- the office will be located in New York.

Nunc congue lorem vitae eros tristique molestie. Maecenas id mauris hendrerit, suscipit lacus et, semper mauris. Sed libero nibh, pharetra id varius vitae, ornare ut ex. Suspendisse potenti.[4]

Flora

Nunc id mollis felis, et placerat felis. Donec porta varius elit non mattis. Morbi pulvinar faucibus volutpat mollis vehicula.

Figure 1. Guernica is a comparatively late example of Cubism. (Pablo Picasso, *Guernica*, 1937, oil on canvas, 11.5 x 25.6 ft (3.49 x 7.76 m), Museo Reina Sofía, Madrid.)

Proin convallis id libero a pharetra. Nullam fringilla, arcu quis vehicula bibendum, eros nulla bibendum magna, quis porttitor leo justo et massa. Duis iaculis viverra arcu, vel aliquam metus

---

4. Violet Wilson, *Songs and Dances of Divinity*, 3rd ed. (Boston: Houghton, 2012), 47.

porta quis. Nunc sit amet ultrices lectus. Interdum et malesuada fames ac ante ipsum primis in faucibus. Proin ultrices eleifend vulputate. Proin a suscipit leo, vel sodales libero. Maecenas ut finibus ligula, eget pulvinar ligula.

Fauna

Vivamus finibus that "dui ut dignissim ultricies, mi arcu tristique ligula, nec luctus tellus diam id quam."[5] Suspendisse aliquet scelerisque rhoncus. Phasellus libero eros, condimentum quis nisl ac, tincidunt lacinia magna.

Table 1. Table title, sentence-style, single-spaced without a period

Stub column head	Spanner head[a]		Spanner head	
	Column head (%)	Column head	Column head (%)	Column head
Stub entry				
Stub subentry	0.00	0.00*	0.00	−.82
Stub subentry	...	...	0.00	−.35
Stub entry				
Stub subentry	0.00	0.00	0.00	1.00
Stub subentry	0.00	0.00	0.00	.98
Stub entry	0.00	0.00*	0.00	.04

Source: Data from Evelyn Henderson, "Effects of Social Networking Sites," *The Washington Post*, January 16, 2020, 12; Wilson, *Divinity*, 49.

Note: General note to the whole table.

[a] Refers to the first part of the research.

* $p < .08$

Vestibulum vitae dictum arcu, sit amet semper lectus. Vestibulum mollis elementum egestas, pharetra. Nunc viverra nunc vel felis bibendum Fringilla fraesent euismod tortor ac lectus cursus, in interdum ex aliquet.[6] Sed pretium magna ac ligula iaculis, id elementum enim dictum arcu

---

5. Evelyn Henderson, "Effects of Social Networking Sites," *The Washington Post*, January 16, 2020, 12.

6. Jeremiah Collins, "Religion and Psychology," *Science* 34, no. 4 (April 2019): 321–29.

odio. Etiam dignissim diam eget eros rhoncus elementum. Nam placerat, dolor in condimentum eleifend, lectus nunc aliquet massa, non porta velit nisl a nibh.

Air Pollution

Donec nec tincidunt neque, id imperdiet purus. Duis ut lectus luctus, pharetra metus eget, dignissim magna. Praesent euismod tortor ac lectus cursus, in interdum ex aliquet. Sed pretium magna ac ligula iaculis, id elementum enim placerat. Nam eget scelerisque massa. Praesent felis enim, gravida vel arcu et, aliquam vulputate diam. Vestibulum ante ipsum primis in faucibus orci luctus et ultrices posuere cubilia curae; Companies scrutinize their business models, break new ground proactively, and develop new skills:

> It is to be expected that digitalization due to performance increase and simultaneous cost reduction will capture all parts of the economy and society. Depending on the point of view digitalization is explained with actual trends which influence patterns of behavior of customers, value-added structures, and the working life. Digitalization is also associated with the challenges and changes that come along for companies.[7]

Aenean pretium non odio at scelerisque. Sed in ante ac massa dignissim sodales. Curabitur elementum rhoncus sem at lobortis maecenas[8] — sollicitudin justo in nunc convallis viverra eget at elit. Integer rhoncus lacus dui, non convallis dolor convallis vitae. Orci varius natoque penatibus et magnis dis parturient montes, nascetur ridiculus mus. Maecenas aliquam ut dui vitae scelerisque.

Atmosphere

Vivamus lectus nulla, ultrices et porta at, imperdiet a ligula. Aliquam ultricies pulvinar maximus. Nulla sodales elit id mauris pretium, id facilisis diam euismod. Fusce eget pharetra sapien. Nulla volutpat viverra urna, nec ornare metus pulvinar ac. Cras et nulla sit amet lorem laoreet pellentesque at eget nunc.[9]

---

7. Wilson, *Divinity*, 46.

8. Wilson, 47.

9. White, "Nonviolence in Action," 49.

Aenean at lectus sem. Vivamus blandit quam et tempus varius. Quisque posuere mi quam, eu tincidunt turpis molestie id. Ut et nibh efficitur, euismod diam in, suscipit tortor. Phasellus ut velit nec sapien posuere consequat ut ac mi.[10]

Pollution Source

Suspendisse nisi arcu, tincidunt a arcu nec, gravida consectetur ipsum. Ut viverra, dolor eget varius aliquam, orci elit mollis sem, non mollis ex mauris eu dui.[11] Vestibulum interdum urna quam, et posuere justo consectetur id. Aliquam sit amet magna rutrum, porttitor tortor ac, ultrices mauris. Alfred Tennyson's "Tears, Idle Tears" is a great example:

> Ah, sad and strange as in dark summer dawns
> . . . .
> The casement slowly grows a glimmering square;
> So sad, so strange, the days that are no more.[12]

Human-made pollution

Fusce tempor placerat lectus. In hac habitasse platea dictumst. Donec vel facilisis dolor, id fermentum dolor. Suspendisse nulla erat, vulputate id ultricies vel, iaculis quis purus. Phasellus tempor magna ac diam tristique, in volutpat nunc imperdiet.[13] Nam vitae enim purus. In hac habitasse platea dictumst. In convallis elit purus, nec condimentum orci lobortis placerat.

Cars. Aenean venenatis lacinia dui a lacinia. Proin placerat non ante sit amet commodo. Praesent dui turpis, tempus eu lorem ac, porttitor venenatis ligula. Curabitur volutpat rutrum commodo, "Suspendisse quam diam, blandit quis ligula nec, tristique faucibus nibh."[14]

---

10. Henry Powell, "Save Water Save Earth," review of *Brave New World*, created by Eleanor Reed, *Signs*, April 9, 2017, http://www.signsog.com/2017/4/9/save_water.

11. Christian Walker, "Centralization and Decentralization," Politics and People, 2011, YouTube Video, 9:42, https://www.youtube.com/watch?v=dsUjd_jf8.

12. Hudson Hayes, email message to author, July 2, 2021.

13. Walker, "Centralization and Decentralization."

14. Henderson, "Social Networking Sites," 12.

Factories. Aenean convallis dapibus dapibus. Sed volutpat, ligula eget interdum bibendum, eros nulla semper nisi, quis commodo enim ante ut enim. Aenean eu pharetra dolor. Donec felis metus, dictum in erat vel, ultrices ultricies ante, "In hac habitasse platea dictumst. Duis leo sem, rutrum in dolor id, vehicula ullamcorper ex. Vivamus non varius lectus."[15]

Natural pollution

Proin dictum varius quam. Proin tempus est id mi condimentum pharetra. Aliquam nisi nunc, tristique at massa in, non viverra condimentum, ante lacus interdum augue, aliquet tempor leo lectus quis tellus. Pellentesque blandit sapien eget ipsum pulvinar molestie. Donec augue orci, congue id leo eu, dignissim blandit felis.

Animals. Vivamus venenatis urna et faucibus consequat. Integer pretium, dui tincidunt rhoncus sagittis, lectus magna mollis nibh, eget hendrerit eros ante ut libero. Nunc ut diam id massa aliquam elementum. Suspendisse potenti. Sed scelerisque sed ante et porta. Vestibulum faucibus aliquet pharetra. Donec ac elementum nunc. Proin congue nisl accumsan elit volutpat efficitur.[16]

Sea salt. Vivamus velit nisi, gravida nec laoreet in, vulputate et tortor. Nulla consequat neque elit, vel accumsan enim tristique nec. Aenean commodo augue vel consectetur molestie. Nam gravida tortor sed pulvinar posuere. Maecenas nisi urna, posuere vel auctor id, auctor sit amet ipsum.

Factors

Nulla aliquet non nulla et gravida. Nunc tincidunt efficitur diam. Nullam molestie libero sed tortor finibus rutrum. Donec ut sodales leo. Nullam scelerisque leo vel bibendum finibus. Donec ut efficitur odio. Nulla molestie, tellus at pretium dapibus, quam neque facilisis lectus, a euismod nisl velit sed tortor.

---

15. "Marriage," *The House on Mango Street*, directed by Camila Turner (1989; Tustin, CA: TusOne Production, 2013), DVD.

16. Sofia Foster, "Effective Ways of Reducing Air Pollution" (PhD dissertation, University of Toronto, 2016), 22–23, http://search.proquest.com/docview/0783574542.

Bibliography

Brooks, James J. *Favorite Athlete*. New York: Pocket Books, 2018.

Collins, Jeremiah. "Religion and Psychology." *Science* 34, no. 4 (April 2019): 321–35.

Foster, Sofia. "Effective Ways of Reducing Air Pollution." PhD dissertation, University of Toronto, 2016. http://search.proquest.com/docview/0783574542.

Henderson, Evelyn. "Effects of Social Networking Sites." *The Washington Post*, January 16, 2020, 12–13.

The House on Mango Street. Directed by Camila Turner. 1989. Tustin, CA: TusOne Production, 2013. DVD.

Picasso, Pablo. *Guernica*. 1937. Oil on canvas, 11.5 x 25.6 ft. (3.49 x 7.76 m). Museo Reina Sofía, Madrid. https://www.museoreinasofia.es/visita/tipos-visita/visita-comentada/guernica-historia-icono.

Powell, Henry. "Save Water Save Earth." Review of *Brave New World*, created by Eleanor Reed. *Signs*, April 9, 2017. http://www.signsog.com/2017/4/9/save_water.

Walker, Christian. "Centralization and Decentralization." Politics and People. 2011. YouTube Video, 9:42. https://www.youtube.com/watch?v=dsUjd_jf8.

White, Mason. "Nonviolence in Action." *Peace Studies*, March 2020, 39–53.

Wilson, Violet. *Songs and Dances of Divinity*. 3rd ed. Boston: Houghton, 2012.